SPRINGTIME in the ROCKIES

Quilts from Rocky Mountain Designers

Konda Luckau

WITH

Emily Herrick

April Mazzoleni

Paula McKinlay

Rebecca Morganson

Machelle Preston

Karlene Riggs

Amy Smart

Margie Ullery

SPRINGTIME in the ROCKIES

Quilts from Rocky Mountain Designers

Konda Luckau

WITH

Emily Herrick, April Mazzoleni, Paula McKinlay, Rebecca Morganson,
Machelle Preston, Karlene Riggs, Amy Smart and Margie Ullery

Editor: Jenifer Dick
Designer: Bob Deck
Photography: Aaron T. Leimkuehler
Illustration: Lon Eric Craven
Technical Editor: Christina DeArmond
Production assistance: Jo Ann Groves

Published by:
Kansas City Star Books
1729 Grand Blvd.
Kansas City, Missouri, USA 64108

All nature photography used in this book comes from the National Park Service photo archives.

First edition, first printing

ISBN: 978-1-61169-055-2

Library of Congress Control Number: 2012941882

Printed in the United States of America by Walsworth Publishing Co., Marceline, MO

To order copies, call StarInfo at (816) 234-4636 and say "Books."

TABLE of CONTENTS

DEDICATION

This book is dedicated to all the amazing quilters who live in the Rocky Mountains.

ACKNOWLEDGEMENTS

The journey to put this book together has certainly been an adventure. The craziness that is called life invaded our deadlines. Among all of us involved, there were births and deaths, weddings and graduations and other sorrows and celebrations. I would like to thank those who helped get this project started, but ended up needing to spend their time elsewhere. I would also like to thank those who were able to help pull this book together and see it through to the end. A special thanks needs to go to Jenifer Dick and The Kansas City Star for their organization and doing all the extra things to make this book what it is. A collaborative book like this takes a lot of coordinating and organizing. Everyone has been wonderful and helpful throughout the process. Thank you again!

INTRODUCTION

Springtime in the Rockies

The perfect spring day in the Rocky Mountains is a rare gift. Generally during what should be spring, winter and summer battle to see who is in charge before summer eventually wins. One day the high temperature will be 40°. The next day it will be 80°, but often it will be 40° and 80° the same day. The rule for gardens is to never plant before Mother's Day. Those who get excited and plant early are more often than not disappointed. We always have a late frost and usually have a late snow.

When I think of spring, I think about color. Blue, not green, is the dominant color of spring here. The deep violet-blue of the mountains is the backdrop of our lives. In the spring, the mountains are still snow-capped, so white is also an important color. I love the blue and white because the rest of our world is brown, dead and bare, from winter's chill. Then slowly, we begin to see green, not a vibrant green like in other parts of the country – we never see that – but a soft, quiet green.

When the green has started replacing the brown, the color comes! First come the brilliant yellow forsythias and the gentle yellow daffodils, then come the colorful tulips and finally the trees erupt in blossoms of soft pink and white. That's when we know spring has arrived. Even though it may be snowing, we know the snow won't last. We savor every day we get that feels like spring!

Springtime in the Rockies contains 15 patterns from 9 designers currently living along the Wasatch Front, as our part of the shadow of the Rocky Mountain Range is called. Just as the perfect spring day is a gift each of us treasure, these projects are our gift to you that we hope you will make and treasure!

THE DESIGNERS

Emily Herrick
Springville, Utah

Emily Herrick is a quilter and the creative force behind **Crazy Old Ladies**. For the past four years she has created innovative quilt patterns from traditional to contemporary that have been featured in a number of international magazines. Her **Crazy Old Ladies** quilt patterns can be found worldwide. Her book **Geared for Guys** features eight up-to-date designs with masculine touches perfect for the guys in your life.

Emily Herrick is also an accomplished fabric designer licensed with Michael Miller Fabrics. To date her collections include: *Going Coastal, Hall of Fame,* and *Shore Thing*.

Emily was born in California and now resides in Utah with her husband, Gilbert, and their three children. To see more of Emily's designs visit www.crazyoldladiesquilts.blogspot.com

Konda Luckau
Payson, Utah

Although Konda's grandmothers and great grandmothers quilted, she never knew them. She learned how to sew in 4-H and Home Economics class and made lots of clothes too embarrassing to wear.

Konda started out her working life as a math teacher. She was introduced to quilting as she was expecting her first child and made a few quilts too embarrassing to use. Then she was introduced to a long arm. It was love at first sight! She started her long arm quilting business, **Moose on the Porch Quilts** about 10 years ago. This evolved into writing patterns a few years later after Konda fell in love with charm squares. Since that time, Konda has 8 books published with patterns for charm squares. She also designs patterns for Northcott, Timeless Treasures, and Moda Bake

Shop. In addition, Konda has had quilts published in *McCall's Quick Quilts, McCall's Quilting, Quiltmaker's 100 Blocks* and *Fat Quarterly*. Her website is www.moosequilts.com.

April Mazzoleni
Payson, Utah

Creativity is something that has been encouraged and handed down for generations in April's family. Whether it is sewing, sketching, music, writing or dreaming, she thinks everyone should create something every day. After relocating from Southern California to Utah with her husband and three children, quilting became a way for her to create and keep her family warm at the same time. Stop by for a visit at www.aprilmaedesigns.com.

Paula McKinlay
Alpine, Utah

A quilt teacher and pattern designer, Paula lives in Alpine, Utah (with a wonderful, understanding family) at the base of some beautiful mountains that tower over their home. She has always loved creating fiber art. She started knitting at age 4, and moved onto creating clothes for her Betsey Wetsey, Barbie and troll doll. She loved making clothes for herself. Her parents bought all the fabric she could sew and also allowed her to wear those creative outfits. Her major in college was pattern drafting.

She and her husband have 5 children, 4 of which are girls, so the creative sewing continues. She has taught 4-H for 33 years and loves to see young girls fall in love with yarns and fabrics. Quilting is an extension of her love of creating and handling fabric. She designed and patterned her first quilt in 2000.

Rebecca Morganson
Payson, Utah

Rebecca Morganson was born and raised in Payson, Utah. She remembers visiting her grandmother while her mom and grandmother quilted for hours. Her job was to keep the needles threaded while she played underneath the quilt. Little did she know then, that this would be the beginning of her love affair with quilting. In 2001, Rebecca and her husband expanded the offerings of their custom picture framing shop to include quilting fabrics. As Rebecca started making displays for the shop, she realized how much she enjoyed the designing process. She now has a large following who eagerly await her next creation. Visit her website at www.stitchesandsewforth.com.

Machelle Preston
Spanish Fork, Utah

Machelle has been interested in textiles since she was a young girl. Her grandmother introduced her to knitting and showed her the world of quilting. The most memorable quilt she made with her grandmother was an appliqué flower girl pattern that was made using cardboard templates and sewn with her sewing machine.

Machelle has always loved to do things with her hands and design many things. She started working with floral arrangements, moved to wood crafts and, now, for the past 12 years has been into quilting. She owned a quilt shop for more than five years, which is now closed. But, Machelle continues to design patterns for local quilt shops, and has had one of her quilts published in *Fons and Porter's Easy Quilts* magazine. Visit her blog at www.cherrytreecottagequilts.blogspot.com.

Karlene Riggs
Spanish Fork, Utah

Karlene's mother taught her to quilt at a very young age. Her sister quilts, her mother-in-law taught quilting classes and her grandmother made hundreds

of quilts in her lifetime, so you could say it's in her blood. She made her first quilt the first year she was married, 21 years ago. About three years ago the local quilt shop owner of Cherry Tree Cottage, saw a few of her quilts and asked her to make store samples. Soon she was working at the store, teaching classes and designing quilts for the store. At age 14, her daughter started making quilts for the same store, continuing the family tradition.

Amy Smart
American Fork, Utah

Amy Smart is a mother to four busy kids and a very patient husband. She's been sewing since childhood and started quilting in earnest after the birth of her first baby, craving something that 'stayed done' in the midst of all those motherhood tasks constantly in need of re-doing. She worked in a local quilt shop for eight years where she began designing patterns. She started writing a blog, *Diary of a Quilter*, three years ago and has thoroughly enjoyed connecting with all the talented and lovely people in the wide quilting world. When she's not sewing or blogging, she can be found volunteering at the kids' schools, watching BBC dramas, and trying not to step on legos. Visit her blog at www.diaryofaquilter.com.

Margie Ullery
Payson, Utah

Margie started playing with fabric when she was a little girl. Her mom was a seamstress and quilter, so there were always scraps to play with. She taught Margie how to sew clothing, piece quilts and hand quilt. She started sewing her own clothes at age 12 and made her first pieced quilt at age 14, which she still has.

She is married and is the mom to five children — one daughter and four very energetic boys. She also enjoys reading, baking, scrapbooking and making jewelry. Visit her blog at www.riboncandyquilts.blogspot.com.

SCRAMBLED EGGS

By Emily Herrick

Finished Quilt Size: 34 ½" x 53"
Finished Block Size: 8 ½" x 11"

"The beautiful blue sky of spring is a welcome sight after the dreary grey skies of the long winter months. I love this very first sign of spring. I can't help but notice the juxtaposition of snowcapped mountains against the blossoming flowers in the valley. Just near my home are farms with cattle, goats and sheep. I love to see the newborn animals as they stand on wobbly legs on their spring birthdays."

– EMILY HERRICK

Fabric Requirements

- 12 fat quarters for eggs and outer border
- 3/4 yard for inner border and binding
- 1 5/8 yard for backing
- 40" x 60" piece of batting

Additional Supplies
Freezer paper

Cutting

- From the border and binding fabric cut:

  - 5 – 2" x the width of fabric strips for inner border

  - 6 – 2 1/2" x the width of fabric strips for the binding

Piecing

The templates are found on pages 80-82.

Trace the egg pattern twice onto the dull side of the freezer paper. Then trace the egg pattern again, once, in reverse. Be sure to label each piece as shown on the pattern. Do not cut pattern pieces apart yet.

Layer 4 fat quarters, right sides up into a stack. Make sure there is plenty of contrast between each print. Press the traced pattern, shiny side down, to the top of the stack making sure there is at least a 2" fabric margin all the way around the template. Reserve the remaining fabric for the outer border.

Rotary cut through the marked lines of the pattern, using a quilting ruler to keep your lines straight. Leave the freezer paper on top of each stack to keep the stacks organized.

Now you will have 12 small stacks labeled A-1 through A-5 and B-1 through B-7. Move the top fabric in stacks A-1 and B-1 to the bottom of their stacks. (Peel the freezer paper off first and place back on top of the stack to help keep pieces in order) Take the top 2 fabric pieces of section B-2 and move to the bottom of the stack, again removing the freezer paper and placing it on the top of the stack.

Begin with Section A and sew the pieces together in numerical order as shown, using a 1/4" seam allowance. The pieces will not match up perfectly and there will be some pieces longer or shorter than the new piece they are being sewn to. Trim each section just enough to get a straight edge before attaching the next piece. Unevenness is normal for blocks pieced in this manner.

Assemble Section B in the same manner.

Sew Section A to Section B. Press. Square-up the block to 9" x 11 1/2". Repeat with the remaining elements to complete the 4 blocks.

Repeat with the remaining 8 fat quarters and 2 traced patterns so you have 8 blocks and 4 blocks reversed.

Top Assembly

Referring to the assembly diagram, lay out the quilt in 3 rows of 4 blocks each. Sew the blocks in order by rows and join the 4 rows together.

Borders

Inner Border

Measure the quilt top center from top to bottom. Sew the inner border strips together and trim to that length. Sew to each side and press. Measure across the top again from side to side and sew the remaining strips that length. Sew one to the top and one to the bottom. Press.

Outer Border

Measure the quilt top center from side to side. Sew the outer border strips together and trim to that length. Sew to each side and press. Measure across the top again from side to side and sew the remaining strips that length. Sew one to the top and one to the bottom. Press.

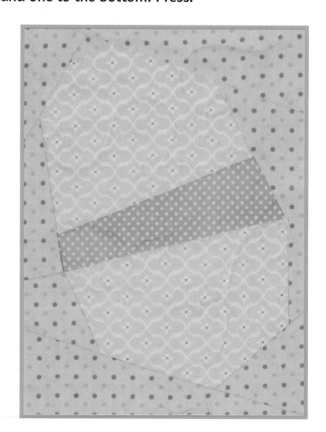

Finishing

Quilt as desired and bind.

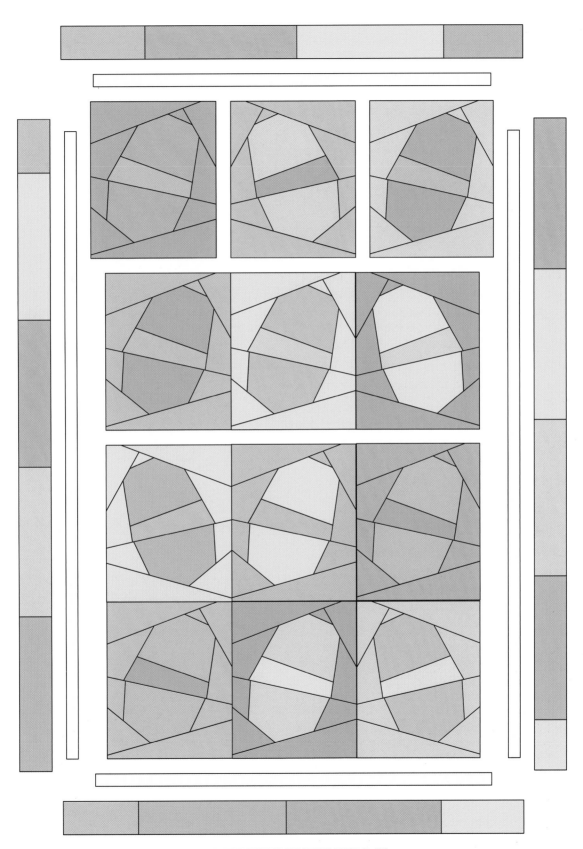

ASSEMBLY DIAGRAM

WILDFLOWERS in BLOOM

By Konda Luckau

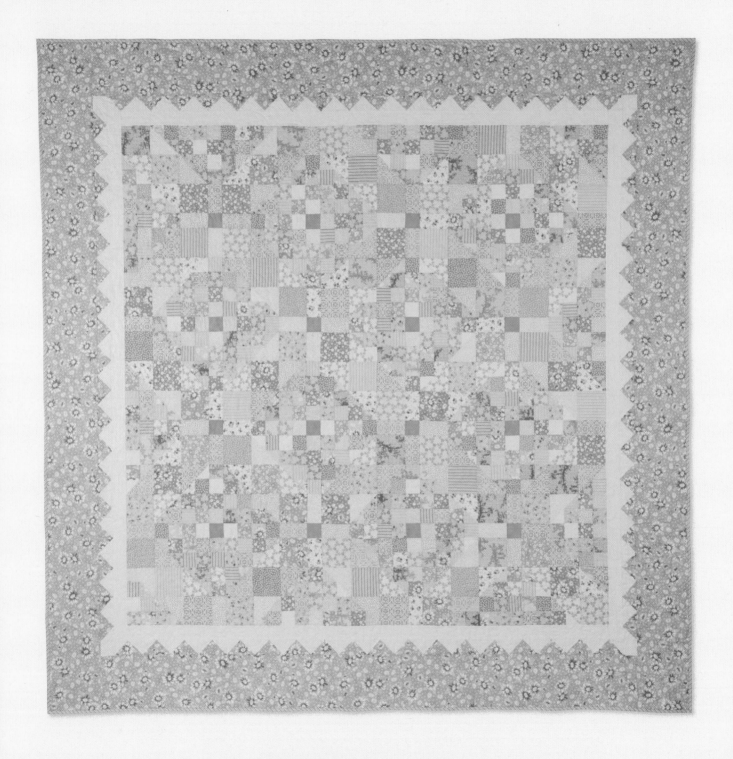

Finished Quilt Size: 90" square
Finished Block Size: 12" square

"When I want to take pictures, I head up the canyon. The mountains are always beautiful. I love seeing them come to life in the spring. Just being in the mountains, I can feel my worries melt away. It is almost magical how comforting it is."

– KONDA LUCKAU

Fabric Requirements

- 12 light fat quarters for large triangles, small triangles and small light squares
- 12 dark fat quarters for the small dark squares and the large dark squares
- 1 fat quarter dark for the sashing cornerstones
- 1 ¼ yards light for the inner border
- 3 yards floral print for the outer border
- 7 yards fabric for the backing
- 1 yard fabric for the binding
- 96" square piece of batting

Cutting

Light Fat Quarters

- From the 12 light fat quarters, cut the following strips x the long side of the fat quarter, approximately 22".

- From 5 light fat quarters cut **each**:
    - 2 – 4 $\frac{7}{8}$" strips (10 total). Sub-cut into 40 – 4 $\frac{7}{8}$" squares and cut each in half diagonally

    - 1 – 4 $\frac{1}{2}$" strip (5 total)

    - 1 – 2 $\frac{1}{2}$" strip (5 total)

- From 1 light fat quarter, cut:
    - 3 – 4 $\frac{7}{8}$" strips. Sub-cut into 12 – 4 $\frac{7}{8}$" squares and cut each in half diagonally

    - 1 - 2 $\frac{1}{2}$" strip

- From the remaining 6 light fat quarters, cut **each**:
    - 7 – 2 $\frac{1}{2}$" strips (42 total) for the small triangles and light squares

    - From the 13 remaining light 2 $\frac{1}{2}$" strips, cut each into 8 - 2 $\frac{1}{2}$" squares (104 total) for the small light triangles.

Dark Fat Quarters

- From 12 dark fat quarters, cut the following strips x the long side of the fat quarter, approximately 22".

    - 35 – 2 $\frac{1}{2}$" strips (3 each from 11 fat quarters and 2 from 1 fat quarter)

    - 19 – 4 $\frac{1}{2}$" strips. Sub-cut into 75 – 4 $\frac{1}{2}$" squares

Sashing Fat Quarters

- From the sashing cornerstone fabric, cut 2 – 2 $\frac{1}{2}$" strips x the width of the fabric. Sub-cut into 16 – 2 $\frac{1}{2}$" squares

Borders

- From the inner border fabric, cut the following strips x the width of the fabric:

    - 8 – 2 $\frac{1}{2}$" strips for the inner border

    - 6 – 2 $\frac{7}{8}$" strips for the pieced border. Sub-cut into 72 – 2 $\frac{7}{8}$" squares and 4 – 2 $\frac{1}{2}$" squares

- From the outer border fabric, cut the following strips x the width of the fabric:

    - 3 – 5 $\frac{1}{4}$" strips for the pieced border. Sub-cut into 18 – 5 $\frac{1}{4}$" squares

    - 9 – 7 $\frac{1}{2}$" strips for the outer border.

Piecing

Sashing

Sew 35 dark 2 $\frac{1}{2}$" strips to the left side of 35 light 2 $\frac{1}{2}$" strips. Press the seam to the dark fabric. Be sure to always sew the dark strip to the left of the light strip. Make 35 strips sets. Reserve 25 for the blocks.

Sew together 10 strip sets in pairs as shown, with the light and dark strips alternating. Make 5.

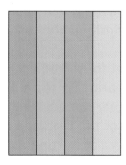

Using the 5 – 4 ½" light strips, sew 1 light 4 ½" strip to the left side of 1 set of strips as shown. Make 5.

Cut each into 8 – 2 ½" x 12 ½" sashing units. Make 40.

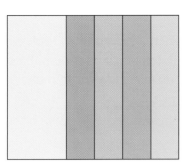

Blocks

Unit A: Triangle Unit

From the remaining 25 strip sets, cut 8 – 2 ½" x 4 ½" pieced units as shown. Use 100 for Unit A, and reserve 100 for Unit B.

Using 100 of the pieced units and the 100 light 2 ½" squares, sew one of the light squares to the dark square as shown. Press. Repeat to make 100 units.

Place one light 4 ⅞" triangle, right sides together, with one unit from above so the corners match as shown. Sew together with a ¼" seam as shown.

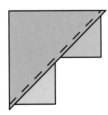

Trim the seam allowance to ¼" and press the seam toward the large triangle. This is unit should measure 4 ½". Repeat to make 100 of Unit A.

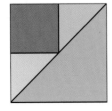

Unit A – 4 ½"
Make 100

Unit B: Four-Patch Unit

Using the remaining 100 pieced units from above, make 50 Four-Patch units.

Randomly match 2 pieced units and sew together to make 1 Four-Patch block as shown. Press. This is unit should measure 4 ½". Repeat to make 50 of Unit B.

Unit B – 4 ½"
Make 50

Block Construction

Using the 100 Unit A, the 50 Unit B, and the 75 dark 4 ½" squares, lay out and assemble one block as shown. Repeat to make 25 – 12 ½" unfinished blocks.

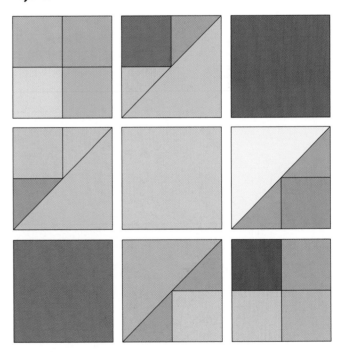

Top Assembly

Lay out the 25 blocks, the 40 sashing units, and the 16 cornerstone squares as shown in the quilt assembly diagram on page 18. Sew into rows. Then sew the rows together to make the quilt center. It should measure 68 ½" square.

Borders

Inner Border

Measure the quilt top center from top to bottom. Sew the 2 ½" inner border strips together and trim to that length and sew to each side. Measure across the top again from side to side and sew 2 strips of the remaining 2 ½" strips that length. Sew one to the top and one to the bottom.

Pieced Border

Using 18 – 5 ¼" outer border squares and 72 – 2 ⅞" inner border squares, make 72 flying geese units.

Draw a diagonal line on the back of all of the 72 – 2 ⅞" inner border squares.

Place two small squares on one large square as shown. Be sure both diagonal lines are matched up. Sew on both sides of the diagonal line then cut apart on the line. Press the seam allowance toward the small squares. This makes two units.

Repeat with all 18 of the 5 ¼" outer border squares and 36 of the 2 ⅞" inner border squares to make 36 of Figure 12.

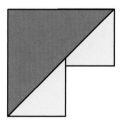

Make 36

Place one of the remaining 2 ⅞" squares in the opposite corner with the diagonal going in the opposite direction as shown. Sew on both sides of the line and cut apart on the line. Press seam allowance towards the small square to make one flying geese unit. Square up to 2 ½" x 4 ½" if necessary. Repeat to make 72 flying geese units.

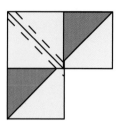

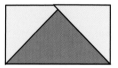

Sew the flying geese together in 4 sets of 18. Sew 2 of these strips onto the left and right sides of the quilt with the inner border fabric next to the inner border as shown in the quilt assembly diagram on page 18.

Sew 1 – 2 ½" inner border square to each ends of the two remaining strips. Sew these strips to the top and bottom of the quilt again with the inner border fabric next to the inner border.

Outer Border

Measure the quilt top center from side to side. Sew the outer border strips together and trim to that length. Sew to each side and press. Measure across the top again from side to side and sew the remaining strips that length. Sew one to the top and one to the bottom. Press.

Finishing

Quilt as desired and bind.

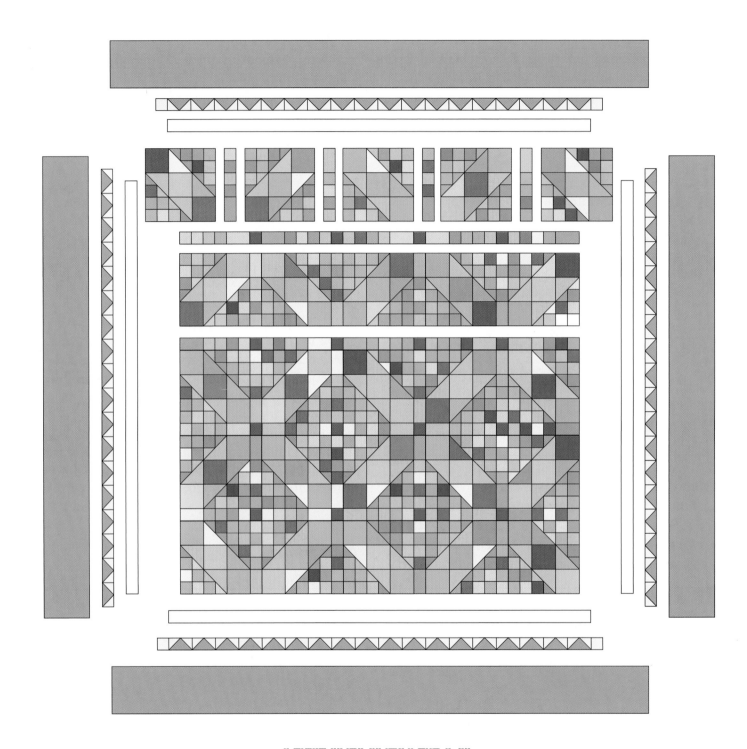

ASSEMBLY DIAGRAM

TRUE NORTH

By Konda Luckau

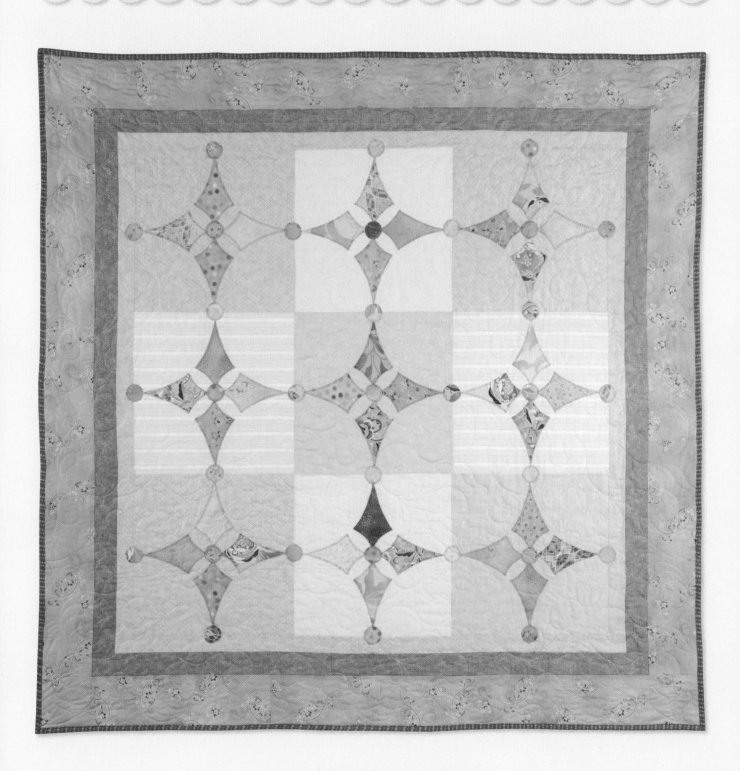

Finished Quilt Size: 57" square
Finished Block Size: 14" square

Fabric Requirements

- 36 – 5" charm squares
- ½ yard of 5 different cream fabrics for the background
- ⅓ yard cream for the inner border
- ⅔ yard brown for the middle border
- 1 yard pink floral for the outer border
- 3 ½ yards for the backing
- ⅔ yard for the binding
- 63" square piece of batting

Additional Supplies
- 1 ⅝ yards of fusible web

Cutting

- From **each** of the ½ yard cream background fabric, cut 2 – 14 ½" squares. There will be one extra.

- From the inner border fabric, cut 5 – 1 ½" x the width of the fabric strips.

- From the middle border fabric, cut 6 – 2 ½" x the width of the fabric strips.

- From the outer border fabric, cut 6 – 5" x the width of the fabric strips.

- From the fusible web, cut 36 – 4 ½" squares.

Appliqué

The templates are found on page 83.

On each square of fusible web, trace 1 circle and 1 wedge from the templates. You need 36 wedges and 33 circles total. Following the manufacturer's instructions, press each 4 ½" square onto the back of one 5" charm square. Cut out the shapes on the lines.

Press 4 wedges and 1 circle onto 1 – 14 ½" background square as shown. Repeat to make 9 blocks. With a coordinating thread color, blanket stitch or zigzag around each wedge and circle.

Borders

Inner Borders

Measure the quilt center from top to bottom. Sew the inner border strips together and trim to that length. Sew to each side and press. Measure across the top again from side to side and sew the remaining strips that length. Sew one to the top and one to the bottom. Press.

Referring to the assembly diagram, press the remaining 24 circles over the seams at the ends of the wedges. Blanket stitch or zigzag around each circle.

Middle Border

Measure the quilt top center from top to bottom. Sew the middle border strips together and trim to that length. Sew to each side and press. Measure across the top again from side to side and sew the remaining strips that length. Sew one to the top and one to the bottom. Press.

Outer Border

Measure the quilt top center from side to side. Sew the outer border strips together and trim to that length. Sew to each side and press. Measure across the top again from side to side and sew the remaining strips that length. Sew one to the top and one to the bottom. Press.

Top Assembly

Lay out the 9 blocks in 3 rows of 3 blocks each. Sew into rows. Then sew the rows together to make the quilt center. It should measure 42 ½" square.

Finishing

Quilt as desired and bind.

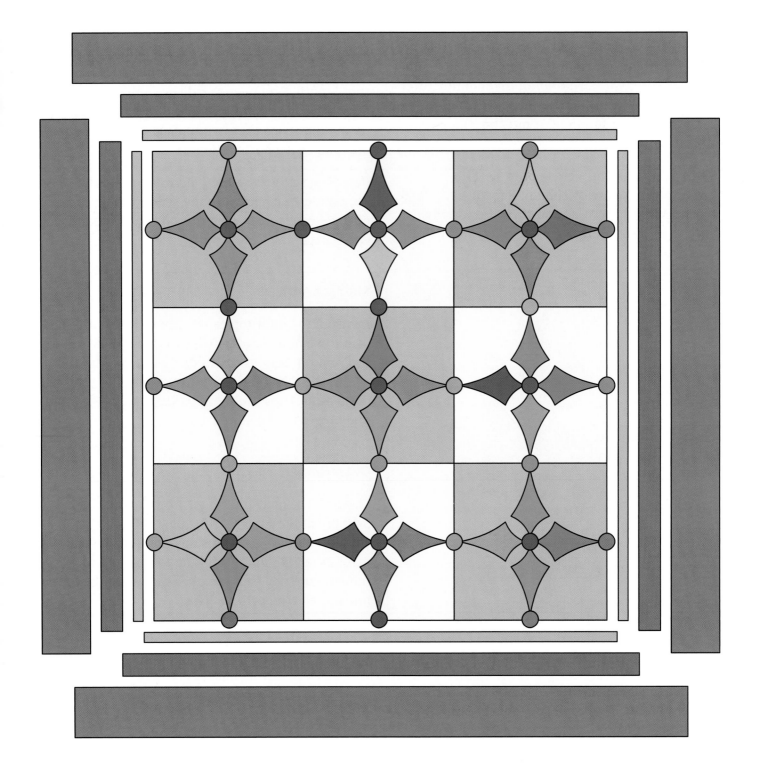

ASSEMBLY DIAGRAM

SPRING BOUQUET

By Konda Luckau

Finished Quilt Size: 20" square
Finished Block Size: 15" square

Fabric Requirements

- ○ 1 fat quarter white for center
- ○ 1 fat quarter for accent border and binding
- ○ Assorted bright scraps
- ○ ²/₃ yard backing fabric
- ○ 24" piece of batting

Additional Supplies
- ○ Watercolor pencils or other coloring supplies like crayons, paints, or fabric markers

Cutting

- From center fabric, cut 1 – 15 ½" square

- From accent border and binding fabric, cut the following strips x the width of the fabric:

  - 4 – 1" strips for the accent border. Cut 2 strips 15 ½" long and cut 2 strips 16 ½" long.

  - 5 – 2 ½" strips for the binding.

- From the assorted bright scraps, cut 36 – 2 ½" squares.

Preparing the Background

The templates are found on pages 84-85.

Trace the quilting design in the middle of the 15 ½" center square using a light box or a window.

Note: If you have a computerized quilting machine, you can download the pattern file from www.moosequilts.com and skip this step.

Borders

Accent Borders

Sew the short accent strips to the sides of the center block as shown in the assembly diagram. Press to the strips. Sew the long accent strips to the top and bottom of the center block. Press to the strips.

Outer Pieced Border

Referring to the diagram lay out the 36 squares in 2 rows of 8 each and 2 rows of 10 each. Make sure the color placement is pleasing to you. When you are happy, stitch the squares together in 4 rows. Press the seams to one side.

Carefully pin the side borders and sew. Press to the accent strips. Repeat with the top and bottom borders. Stay stitch ⅛" around the entire top.

Quilting

Layer the top with batting and backing. Quilt the flower bouquet in either a coordinating or contrasting thread. Quilt the borders as desired. Bind the quilt.

Finishing

Color the flower bouquet using the watercolor pencils or other medium of your choice. Using a pressing cloth, press to heat set the color.

ASSEMBLY DIAGRAM

JOSEFINA and HER DRESS of MANY COLORS

By April Mazzoleni

Finished Quilt Size: 21" x 23"

"Springtime in the mountains is a magical time of year. When I drive to my favorite quilt shop, I always take the back road that runs along some local farm land. The green pastures blend seamlessly into the green mountains surrounding the valley. That is when I take a deep breath and remember how blessed I am to live in such a beautiful area."

— APRIL MAZZOLENI

Fabric Requirements

- ¼ yard of 4 different white fabrics for the background
- ½ yard of light blue print for the border and binding
- ⅛ yard of assorted colors of 9 different fabrics or the equivalent of scraps for Josefina's dress
- Muslin scraps for face and arms
- Wool or Felt for Josefina's hair
- ¾ yard for the backing
- 27" x 29" piece of batting

Additional Supplies
- Fusible web
- Pink crayon

Cutting

- From **each** white background fabric, cut 1 – 8 ½" x 9 ½" rectangle.

- From the light blue border fabric, cut 2 – 3" x 18 ½" strips and 2 – 3" x 21 ½" strips.

- Choose one of the ⅛ yard cuts for the bodice of Josefina's dress. Set aside enough of this fabric for the bodice. Use the template found on page 86 to determine this size.

- From **each** ⅛ yard dress fabrics (including the leftover from the bodice), cut 1 – 2" strip x the width of the fabric (9 strips total).

Background and Borders

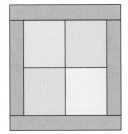

Sew the white background rectangles together into a 16 ½" x 18 ½" four-patch block. Sew the 18 ½" border strips to either side and the 21 ½" border strips to the top and bottom.

Josefina's Dress

When sewing the skirt portion of Josefina's dress, you will be making a mini quilt. This goes faster if you strip piece this portion of the quilt, or you can piece the quilt one square at a time if you are using scraps.

To strip piece, sew the 9 – 2" strips of dress fabric into 3 sets of 3.

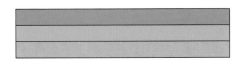

Cut these sections into 2" segments.

Sew these segments into 9 nine-patch units. You can create a pattern or vary your blocks for a scrappy look.

Sew the nine-patch units together to create your mini quilt as shown. This mini quilt will act as one piece of fabric that you will use to cut the dress appliqué from.

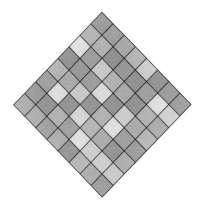

Appliqué

The templates are found on pages 86-87.

Following the manufacturer's instructions on the fusible web, trace and cut out the following appliqué pieces.

- Head and arms from the muslin
- Hair from the wool or felt
- Bodice from bodice print
- Dress Skirt from the mini quilt. Lay the mini quilt on point in order to fit the skirt appliqué pattern.

Trace the face onto the right side of the Head. Color the lips and cheeks lightly with a pink crayon. Heat set the crayon by pressing with a hot iron, placing a piece of paper between the fabric and the iron.

Referring to the placement diagram on page 30, attach the appliqué pieces to the quilt top and top stitch down. Be sure the bottom of her skirt just touches the bottom border so Josefina is standing rather than floating. To achieve the look shown, top stitch in black going along each piece three times. For a different look, use a zigzag, buttonhole stitch or any other decorative stitch.

Finishing

Quilt as desired and bind.

ASSEMBLY DIAGRAM

The HILLS are ALIVE By April Mazzoleni

Finished Quilt Size: 21" square

Fabric Requirements

- ⅛ yard of 7 different blues. One will be for the border.
- ⅛ yard of 5 different greens. One will be for the border.
- ⅛ yard of white
- Scraps of green, yellow and pink for the flower
- 25" square for the backing
- ¼ yard for the binding

Additional Supplies

- Light- to medium-weight fusible interfacing

Background Blocks

Set aside the 2 fabrics you have chosen for the border.

Label all of your blues 1-6 with 1 being the darkest and 6 being the lightest. Label all of your greens 1-4 with 1 and 3 being the lighter two and 2 and 4 being the darker two.

The background of this quilt is made up of 9 log cabin blocks, 6 for the sky and 3 for the hill.

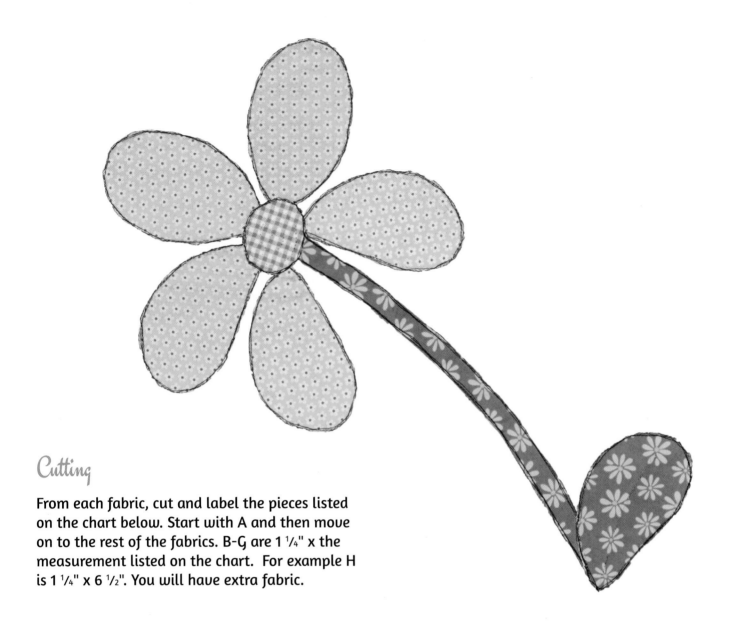

Cutting

From each fabric, cut and label the pieces listed on the chart below. Start with A and then move on to the rest of the fabrics. B-G are 1 ¼" x the measurement listed on the chart. For example H is 1 ¼" x 6 ½". You will have extra fabric.

	A 2" x 2"	B 2"	C 2 ¾"	D 3 ½"	E 4 ¼"	F 5 ¾"	G 5"	H 6 ½"
Blue 1	1		1	1	1	1	1	1
Blue 2		1	1	1	1	1	1	
Blue 3	2		2	2	2	2	2	2
Blue 4		2	2	2	2	2	2	
Blue 5	3		3	3	3	3	3	3
Blue 6		3	3	3	3	3	3	
Green 1		1			1	3		3
Green 2			1	1	3		3	
Green 3			3	3				
Green 4	3					1	1	
White		2	2	2	2	2	2	

Blocks

Sky Blocks

Referring to the diagrams, sew the strips into log cabin blocks starting with the center A square and working your way out.

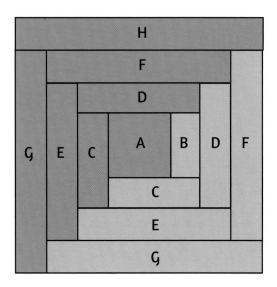

Make:
1 – Blue 1/Blue 2 Block
2 – Blue 3/Blue 4 Blocks
3 – Blue 5/Blue 6 Blocks

Hill Blocks

The hill blocks will be sewn in the same manner using green and white. Use the color reference below to lay out your blocks, and then sew the pieces together in the same order as before.

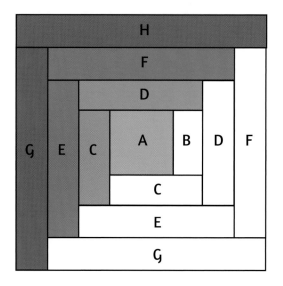

Make:
2 - Green/White blocks

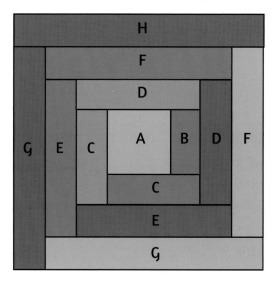

Make:
1 - Green/Green Block

Sewing

Top Assembly

Referring to the assembly diagram, sew the 9 blocks together in 3 rows with 3 blocks each. Make sure you have the blocks placed in the proper position so you can see the sky and hill clearly.

Borders

- From **each** of the border fabrics, cut 1 – 2" x 18 ½" strip and 1 – 2" x 21 ½" strip.

Sew the short blue strip to the left side of the top and the short green to the right side. Press. Then sew the long blue strip to the top and the long green strip to the bottom. Press.

Appliqué

Flower Stem

From the green scrap, cut 1 – 2" x 11" strip. Fold it in half lengthwise and press with wrong sides together to make the strip ½" x 11". Referring to the photo of the quilt, pin this strip to your quilt top making sure that the side of the strip with the raw edge is against the quilt top.

Flower and Leaf

The templates are found on page 88.

Using fusible web and following the manufacturer's instructions, trace and cut out the following appliqué pieces:

- 1 – Pink Flower Center
- 2 – Yellow Flower A reversed
- 1 – Yellow Flower A
- 1 – Green Flower A for the leaf
- 2 – Yellow Flower B

Referring to the photo of the quilt for placement, attach all of the appliqué pieces to the quilt top and top stitch down. To achieve the look shown, top stitch in black going along each piece three times. For a different look, use a zigzag, buttonhole stitch or any other decorative stitch.

Finishing

Quilt as desired and bind.

ASSEMBLY DIAGRAM

SWEET and SIMPLE
By Paula McKinlay

Quilt Size: 41" square
Finished Block Size: 3" square

"My home in Alpine is nestled in the corner and at the base of the rugged Rockies. Each year I watch out my windows as the snowcapped winter melts into spring. This majestic view inspires my work. My mountain home gives me strength, protection and a pastel palette for my quilts."

– PAULA McKINLAY

Fabric Requirements

- 1 yard total of medium to bold scraps for blocks
- ³/₄ yard light for background
- ³/₄ yard medium-light for background
- ⁵/₈ yard for borders
- 1 ¼ yards fabric for backing
- ½ yard fabric for binding
- 45" square piece of batting

Cutting

- From the light background fabric, cut 120 – 2 ³/₈" squares. Cut each in half on the diagonal to make 240 triangles.

- From the medium-light background fabric, cut 122 – 2 ³/₈" squares. Cut each in half on the diagonal to make 244 triangles.

- From the medium to bold fabric scraps, cut 121 – 2 ⁵/₈" squares.

- From the border fabric, cut 4 – 4 ½" strips x the width of the fabric.

Blocks

Sew 4 light triangles to all 4 sides of 60 of the 2 ⁵/₈" squares. Press to the triangles. Make 60.

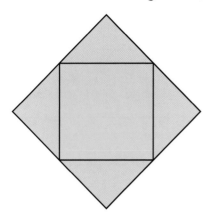

Repeat with the remaining 2 ⁵/₈" squares and the medium-light triangles. Make 61.

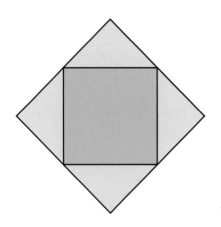

Top Assembly

Referring to the assembly diagram, alternate the light and medium light backgrounds, lay out the 121 blocks in 11 rows of 11 blocks each.

Sew into rows, and sew the rows together to make the top. Press.

Borders

This quilt has mitered borders because of the striped border fabric. You may miter yours if you also use striped fabric or use straight borders as described here.

Measure the quilt top center from top to bottom. Sew the 4 ½" border strips together and trim to that length. Sew to each side and press. Measure across the top again from side to side and sew the remaining 4 ½" strips that length. Sew one to the top and one to the bottom. Press.

Finishing

Quilt as desired and bind.

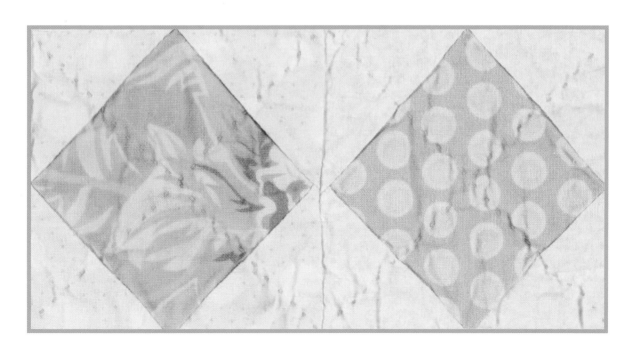

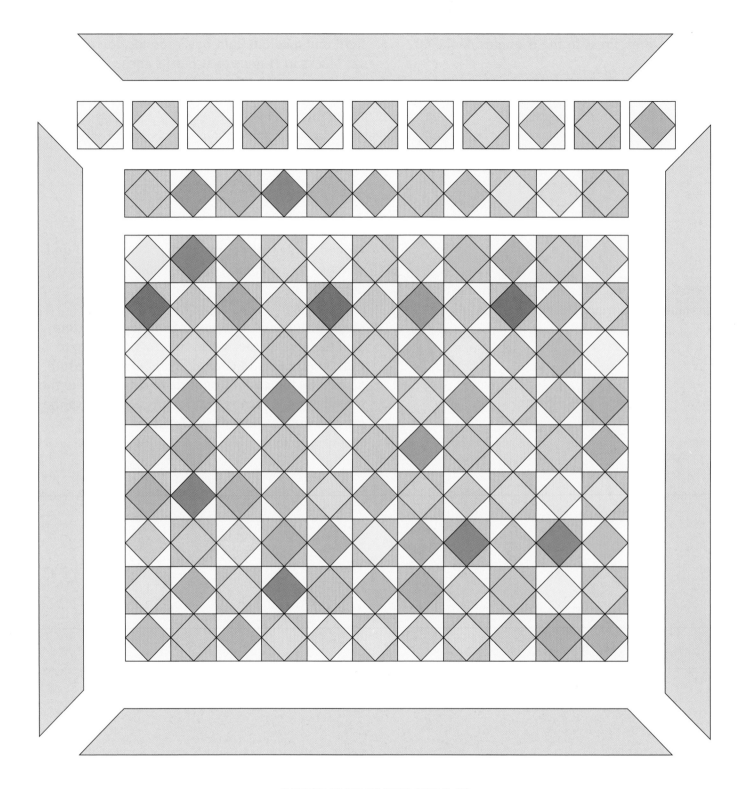

ASSEMBLY DIAGRAM

TINY PATHS
By Paula McKinlay

Quilt Size: 42" square
Finished Block Size: 6" square

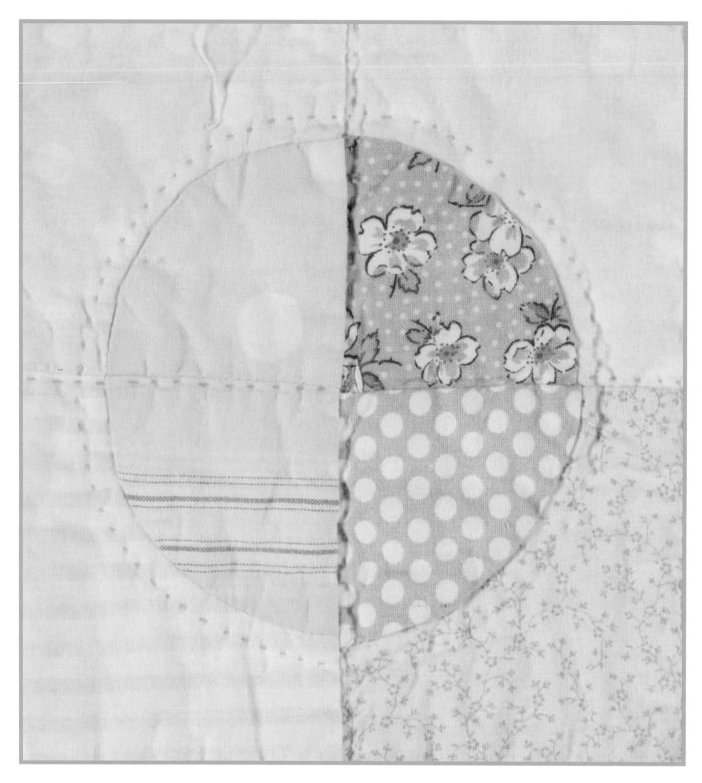

Fabric Requirements

- ○ 1 ½ yards total of light scraps
- ○ 1 ¼ yards total of medium to bold scraps
- ○ ½ yard border fabric
- ○ 1 ¼ yards fabric for backing
- ○ ½ yard fabric for binding
- ○ 45" square piece of batting

Cutting

The templates are found on page 89.

Each unit is two parts, the small quarter circle, or convex piece, and the large background, or concave, piece. Using the templates cut the following:

- From light fabric, cut 144 concave pieces.

- From medium and bold fabrics, cut 144 convex pieces.

- From border fabric cut 4 – 3 ½" strips the width of the fabric.

Blocks

Pin together a convex piece and a concave piece using 3 pins – one at the beginning, middle and end of seam. When pinning, take the tiniest "bite" of fabric, so the seam is not distorted. To sew the block, place the convex piece on the top and ease in as stitching. Press the seam toward the convex piece. Each unit will be 3 ½" unfinished. Repeat to make 144 units.

Lay out the units in groups of 4 and sew together as shown. Make 36 blocks.

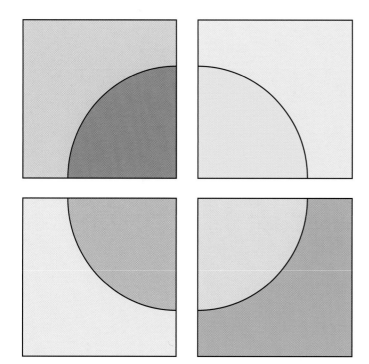

Top Assembly

Referring to the assembly diagram, arrange the blocks as desired in 6 rows of 6. Sew the blocks into rows and then join the rows to complete the quilt top center.

Borders

This quilt has mitered borders because of the striped border fabric. You may miter yours if you also use striped fabric or use straight borders as described here.

Measure the quilt top center from top to bottom. Trim two border strips to that length. Sew to each side and press. Measure across the top again from side to side and cut the remaining strips that length. Sew one to the top and one to the bottom. Press.

Finishing

Quilt as desired and bind.

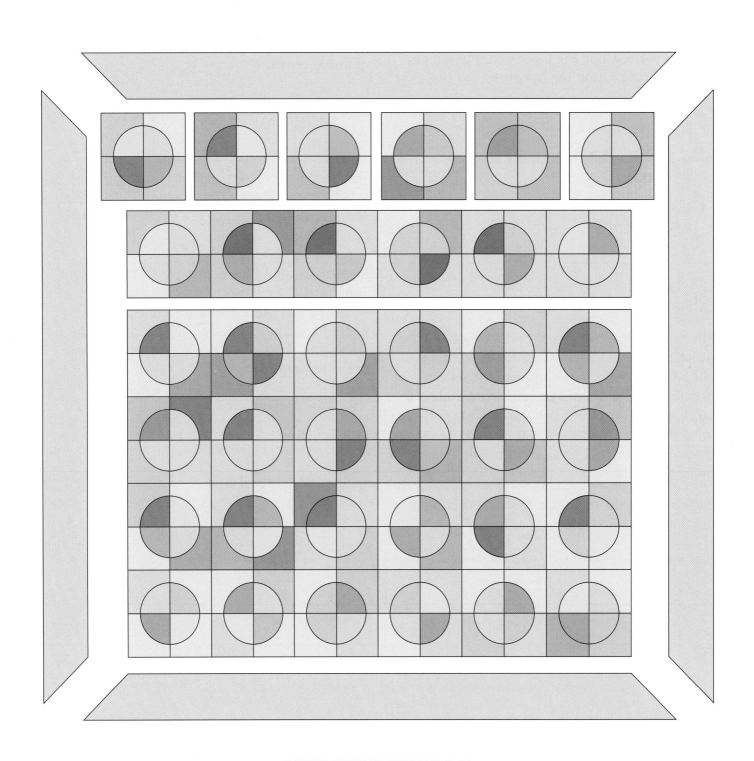

ASSEMBLY DIAGRAM

SPRINGTIME in the ROCKIES

OVER the GARDEN WALL

By Rebecca Morganson

Finished Quilt Size: 67 ½" x 78 ½"

"I love when springtime comes to our little valley nestled in the heart of the Rocky Mountains. As fruit trees bloom in the orchards surrounding our little farm, I am filled with anticipation and hope of things to come. The mountains around us bring a feeling of warmth and security – just like a cozy old quilt."

– REBECCA MORGANSON

Fabric Requirements

- 1 ⅓ yards for appliqué background
- ⅔ yard green for appliqué vines and leaves
- 13 coordinating fat quarters for blocks and flower appliqué
- ⅝ yard for inner border
- 1 ¼ yards for outer border
- 4 yards for backing ⅔ yard for binding
- 73" x 84" piece of batting

Additional Supplies
1 ¼ yards of light- to medium-weight fusible interfacing

Cutting

- From the background fabric, cut 6 – 7 ½" strips x the width of fabric.

- From the 13 fat quarters, cut a total of:
  - 44 – 4 ½" x 8 ½" rectangles
  - 20 – 4 ½" squares
  - 80 – 2 ½" squares – cut in sets of 2 of the same color
  - Reserve the rest for the appliqué

- From the first border fabric, cut 7 – 2" x the width of fabric strips.

- From the final border fabric, cut 7 – 6" x the width of fabric strips.

- From the binding fabric, cut 8 – 2 ½" x the width of the fabric strips.

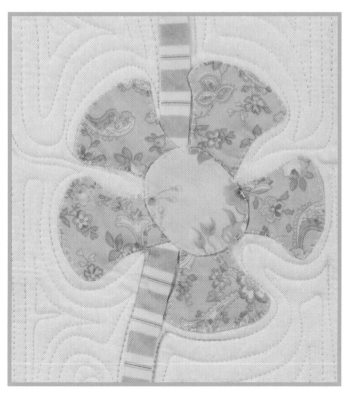

Pieced Rows

Sew two contrasting 2 ½" squares together. Repeat using the same colors. Press both toward the darker fabric.

Flip one of the units and sew together to create the four-patch. Be careful to align the seams.

Repeat to make 20 Four-Patch units.

Sew each Four-Patch unit to a 4 ½" square. Press toward the square. Repeat to create 20 units.

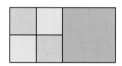

From the 44 – 4 ½" x 8 ½" rectangles, piece the following units:

- From 24 rectangles, sew 12 units of 2 rectangles each

- From 18 rectangles, sew 6 units of 3 rectangles each

- Two will remain as single units

Pieced Row Assembly

Referring to the quilt assembly diagram, make 4 rows using the 42 units and the four-patch units. Each row should measure 8 ½" x 64 ½". You can follow the diagram exactly or arrange them in your own pleasing way.

Appliqué

Background

Prepare the appliqué backgrounds by sewing 2 – 7 ½" background strips together end to end. Trim to 64 ½". Repeat to make 3 rows.

Bias Stems

Cut 1 ¾" bias strips from the vine fabric. Join them to create 3 strips, each measuring 75".

Fold the background strips in half lengthwise with the wrong sides together. Using a lead pencil or fabric marking pen draw a gently waving line through the length of each of the appliqué background strips.

Place the raw edge of the folded vine on the marked line. Using a **scant** ¼ inch seam sew the vine strip to the background fabric. Bend the folded edge of the vine over the stitching line, making sure to cover the seam allowance. Press and stitch along the folded edge to secure. Trim any excess at the ends even with the background fabric.

Leaves and Flowers

The templates are found on page 89.

Trace the appliqué shapes onto the non-fusible side of the interfacing. Cut out leaving about ½" of interfacing around the shapes. Place the fusible side of the shapes to the right side of fabric. Sew on the traced line and then cut about ³⁄₁₆" from the line. Cut a small slit in the center of the interfacing and turn the appliqués right side out. Finger press the edges making sure the interfacing is tucked under the fabric.

Arrange 3 large flowers along each vine and then fill in with the heart buds and leaves. Refer to the photo or quilt assembly diagram for suggested placement. When the appliqué is positioned to your liking, fuse in place with a hot iron. Steam helps to pull the interfacing tight. Using a buttonhole stitch, sew the appliqué in place to secure.

Top Assembly

Referring to the assembly diagram, arrange and sew the rows together, alternating the pieced and appliquéd rows. Begin and end with a pieced row.

Borders

Inner Border

Measure the quilt top center from top to bottom. Sew the inner border strips together and trim to that length. Sew to each side and press. Measure across the top again from side to side and sew the remaining strips that length. Sew one to the top and one to the bottom. Press.

Outer Border

Measure the quilt top center from side to side. Sew the outer border strips together and trim to that length. Sew to each side and press. Measure across the top again from side to side and sew the remaining strips that length. Sew one to the top and one to the bottom. Press.

Finishing

Quilt as desired and bind.

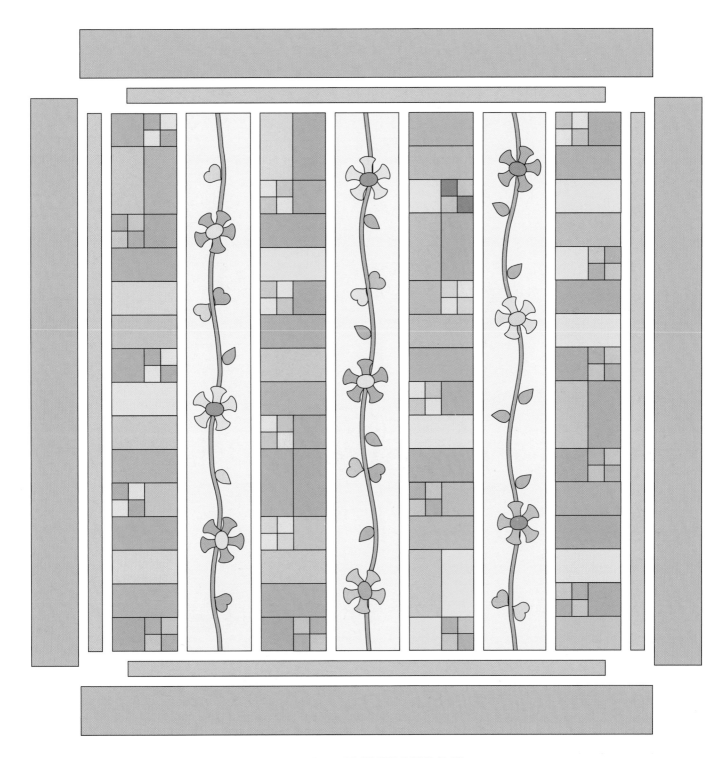

ASSEMBLY DIAGRAM

FRESH CUT FLOWERS

By Rebecca Morganson

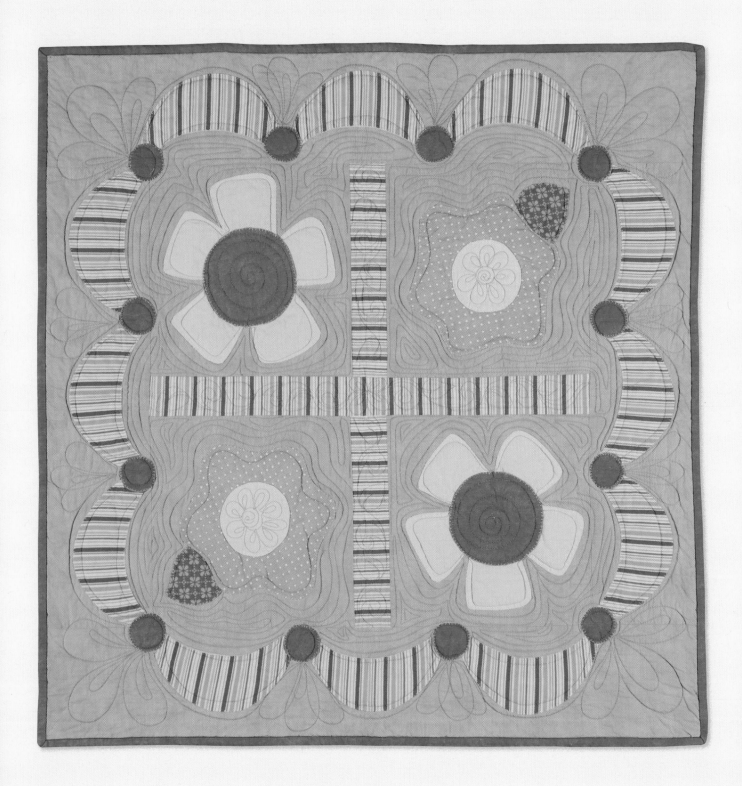

Finished Quilt Size: 34" square

Fabric Requirements

- 1 ⅓ yard for background and border
- ½ yard for sashing and scallops
- ¼ yard for center of flowers and circles on swags
- 2 different fat quarters for flowers
- Scrap of green for leaves
- ⅓ yard for binding
- 1 ⅛ yard for backing
- 40" square piece of batting

Additional Supplies
- 2 ¼ yards light- to medium-weight fusible interfacing

Cutting

- From the background fabric, cut 4 – 11" squares.

- From the border fabric, cut 4 – 6" x the width of fabric strips.

- From the sashing fabric, cut 2 – 2 ½" x 11" strips and 1 – 2 ½" x 23 ½" strip.

- From the binding fabric, cut 4 – 2 ½" x the width of the fabric strips.

Appliqué

The templates are found on pages 90-91.

Using the templates trace 2 of each flower, 2 leaves, 12 swags and 12 circles onto the non-fusible side of the fusible interfacing. Be sure to leave at least 1" between tracings.

Cut the traced images apart about ½" outside of the drawn line. Place one at a time on the appropriate fabric. The fusible side of interfacing should be against the right side of fabric.

Sew on the traced line. Trim the seam allowance to a little more than ⅛" from the stitching. Cut a slit in the interfacing. Turn the appliqué piece right side out through the slit. Finger press and repeat with all other pieces.

Place the flower pieces onto background blocks and press, using steam, to bond. Machine or hand stitch to secure flowers.

Top Assembly

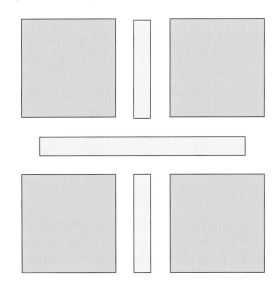

Arrange the 4 appliquéd blocks in 2 rows of 2. Sew the short sashing strips between the blocks and press. Join the two rows with the long sashing strip and press.

Borders

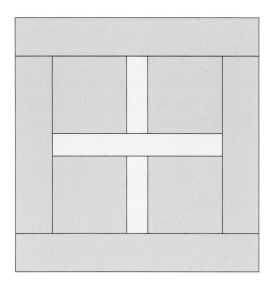

Measure the quilt top center from top to bottom. Sew the 6" border strips together and trim to that length. Sew to each side and press. Measure across the top again from side to side and sew the remaining strips that length. Sew one to the top and one to the bottom. Press.

Referring to the assembly diagram, arrange the swags on the borders. Add a circle in between each swag. Press and stitch in place to secure.

Finishing

Quilt as desired and bind.

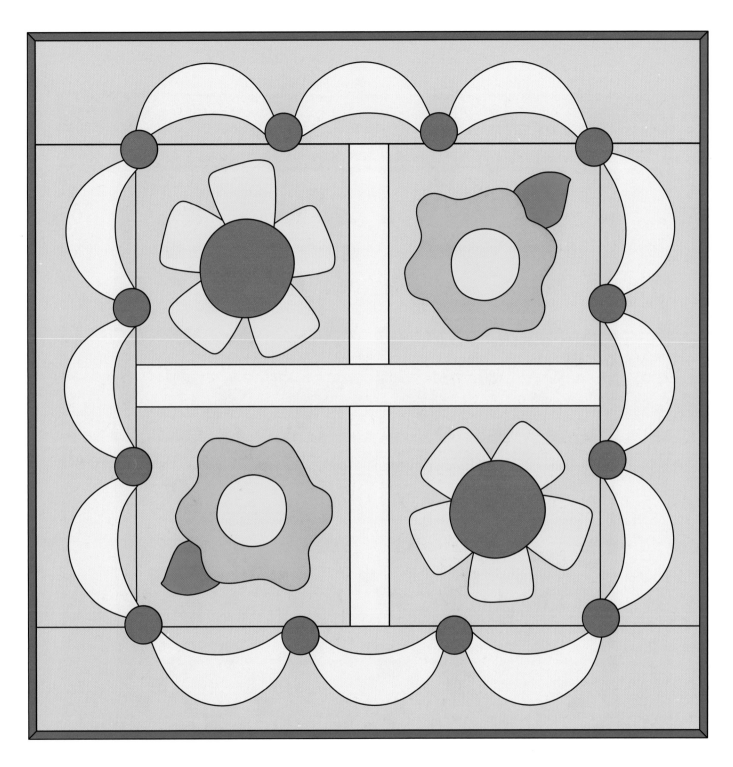

ASSEMBLY DIAGRAM

SPRINGTIME in the ROCKIES 53

STEPPING into SPRING

By Machelle Preston

Finished Quilt Size: 70" x 82"
Finished Block Size: 6"

"The Rocky Mountains are majestic and beautiful, and I feel peace and security living right next to them. As I traveled the world over, I came back to live right next to these beautiful large protecting mountains. Here I feel safe and secure."

– MACHELLE PRESTON

Fabric Requirements

- 3 ¼ yards total of 4 different white on white fabrics
- 2 ½ yards total of 2 medium blues and 1 dark blue
- ⅛ yard each of 3 different yellows
- Scraps of green for the appliqué stem and leaves
- ¾ yard of dark blue for the inner border
- ½ yard of yellow for the middle border
- 1 ½ yard of a floral for the outer border
- 4 ¼ yards for backing
- ¾ yard of blue for binding

Additional Requirements

- DMC Floss: 90, 322, 3346, 3348, 3031

Cutting

- From the white fabrics, cut:
  - 1 – 18 ½" strip x the width of fabric and sub-cut into 1 – 18 ½" square and 2 – 7" squares
  - 13 – 2 ½" strips x the width of fabric
  - 7 – 6 ½" strips x the width of fabric and sub-cut into 42 – 6 ½" squares

- From the blue fabrics, cut:
  - 1 – 7" strip x the width of fabric and sub-cut into 2 – 7" squares
  - 1 – 6 ½" strips x the width of fabric and sub-cut into 4 – 6 ½" squares
  - 22 – 2 ½" strips x the width of fabric
    - From 11 strips, sub-cut 168 – 2 ½" squares
    - set aside 11 strips for strip sets

- From each of the three yellow fabrics, cut:
  - 1 – 2 ½" strip x the width of fabric (3 total)

- From the dark blue border fabric cut 7 – 2 ½" strips x the width of fabric

- From the yellow border fabric cut 7 – 1 ½" strips x the width of fabric

- From floral border print cut 8 – 5 ½" strips x the width of fabric

Piecing

Center Appliqué Block

The templates are found on pages 78-79.

Draw a diagonal line on the back of the 4 blue 6 ½" squares. Place one of these squares in the corner of the 18 ½" white square. Sew on the line and trim seam allowance to ¼".

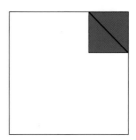

Press the seam allowance to the outside.

Repeat, sewing a blue square into all 4 corners of the center square.

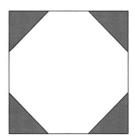

Center the appliqué pattern on the block. Trace the design with an appliqué pencil using the window or a light box to transfer pattern. Use your favorite method of appliqué for petals, stems leaves. Embroider smaller grass and flowers using 3 strands of embroidery floss following the colors on the pattern.

Nine-Patch Blocks

Make 44

Using the 2 ½" strips, make 5 strips sets as shown in the diagram with the colored strips being placed randomly on both sides of a white strip. Mix the strips so each one is different.

Using the remaining 8 white strips, 1 yellow strip, and 3 blue strips, make 4 strips sets as shown with the colored strips being placed between two white strips.

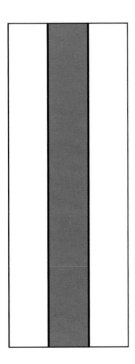

Sub-cut each strip set into 2 ½" sections.

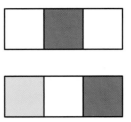

Sew the 2 ½" sections into 44 Nine-Patch Blocks. Make 14 blocks with 5 white squares, and 30 blocks with 5 colored squares.

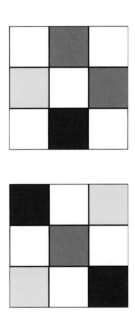

Snowballs Blocks

Make 42

Using the 42 – 6 ½" white squares and the 168 – 2 ½" blue squares, make 42 snowball blocks as shown in the Center Appliqué Block instructions.

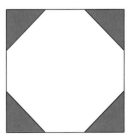

Half-Square Triangle Block

Make 4

Draw a diagonal line on the back of 2 – 7" white squares. Match them and the 2 – 7" blue fabrics, right sides together, and sew ¼" from both sides of the line.

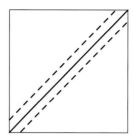

Cut on the line and press to the dark. Trim to 6 ½" square.

Top Assembly

Referring to quilt assembly diagram, layout blocks according to diagram. Sew together.

Complete until all rows are sewn together.

Borders

Inner Border

Measure the quilt top center from top to bottom. Sew the inner border strips together and trim to that length. Sew to each side and press. Measure across the top again from side to side and sew the remaining strips that length. Sew one to the top and one to the bottom. Press.

Middle Border

Measure the quilt top center from top to bottom. Sew lengths of the 1 ½" yellow middle border strips that length and sew to each side. Measure across the top again from side to side and sew lengths of the remaining strips that length. Sew one to the top and one to the bottom.

Outer Border

Measure the quilt top center from side to side. Sew the outer border strips together and trim to that length. Sew to each side and press. Measure across the top again from side to side and sew the remaining strips that length. Sew one to the top and one to the bottom. Press.

Finishing

Quilt as desired and bind.

ASSEMBLY DIAGRAM

GRANDMA'S TULIP GARDEN

By Karlene Riggs

Finished Quilt Size: 48" square
Finished Block Size: 8"

"My inspiration is the mountains — our Rocky Mountains. I love their colors in the springtime and the sounds of the birds singing from their trees. When I look at them, they remind me of my family who has lived alongside them for generations. I love the feeling of security from the mountains, of knowing my family is close and I will always have something to lean upon."

– KARLENE RIGGS

Fabric Requirements

- 2 yards assorted brown for backgrounds and outer border
- 1 yard assorted pink for appliqué and outer border
- ¼ yard assorted green for appliqué
- ¼ yard pink for inner border
- ¾ yard brown print for middle border and binding
- 3 yards for backing
- 52" square piece of batting

Additional Supplies
- Fusible web

Cutting

- From the assorted brown block background fabric, cut:
    - 48 – 2 ½" squares
    - 12 – 2 ½" x 8 ½" strips
    - 14 medium brown 5" squares
    - 14 dark brown 5" squares
- From the assorted brown setting triangle fabric, cut:
    - 2 – 12 ½" squares. Cut each of these squares with an X diagonally for a total of 8 triangles for the side setting triangles
    - 2 – 6 ½" squares. Cut each of these squares on the diagonal once for a total of 4 triangles for the corner setting triangles.
- From the pink inner border fabric, cut 4 strips 1 ½" x the width of fabric
- From the brown middle border and binding fabric, cut 9 strips 2 ½" x the width of fabric
- From the assorted pink outer border fabrics, cut 22 – 5" squares
- From the assorted brown outer border fabrics, cut 22 – 5" squares

Blocks

Block 1

Sew 4 assorted brown 2 ½" x 8 ½" strips as shown, to make 1 – 8 ½" unfinished square block. Press. Make 3.

Block 1 Make 3

Block 2

Sew 16 assorted brown 2 ½" squares in 4 rows of 4 blocks each. Press each row in the opposite direction. Sew the rows together to make 1 – 8 ½" unfinished square block. Press. Make 3.

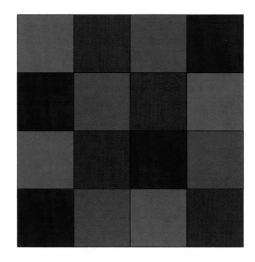

Block 2 Make 3

Block 3

Each Block 3 is made of 4 half-square triangle units that are half medium brown and half dark brown.

On the back of the 5" medium brown square, draw a diagonal line from corner to corner. Place this square, right sides together, with a 5" dark brown square. Sew ¼" on both sides of the line. Cut apart on the drawn line and press open. Trim the unit to 4 ½" square. Repeat to make 4 units.

Lay out the 4 squares with the medium brown facing to the center of the block as shown. Sew together to make 1 – 8 ½" square block. Press. Make 3.

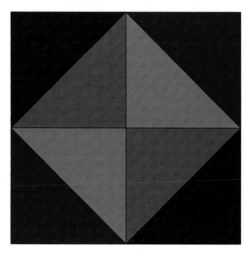

Block 3 Make 3

Block 4

Each Block 4 is made of 4 half-square triangle units that are half medium brown and half dark brown. Use the directions from Block 3 to make 4 assorted medium brown/dark brown half-square triangle units.

Lay out the 4 squares like a pinwheel as shown, alternating the medium and dark browns. Sew together to make 1 – 8 ½" square block. Press. Make 4.

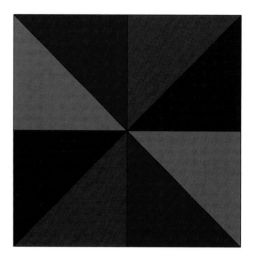

Block 4 Make 4

Appliqué

The templates are found on page 92.

Following directions on the fusible web package, trace the template 13 times. Iron the tulips, leaves and stems to the 13 blocks. Stitch in place as desired.

Top Assembly

Referring to the quilt assembly diagram on page 65, lay out the 13 blocks, 8 quarter square side setting triangles, and 4 half-square corner triangles in diagonal rows. Sew each row together, pressing in opposite directions. Sew rows together. Press.

Inner Border

Measure the quilt top center from top to bottom. Trim 2 inner border strips to that length. Sew to each side and press. Measure across the top again from side to side and cut the remaining strips that length. Sew one to the top and one to the bottom. Press.

Middle Border

Measure the quilt top center from side to side. Trim 2 middle border strips to that length. Sew to each side and press. Measure across the top again from side to side and cut the remaining strips that length. Sew one to the top and one to the bottom. Press.

Outer Border

The outer border is made of 44 half-square triangle units. Referring to the instructions in Block 3, make 44 half-square triangle units from the 22 pink and 22 brown 5" squares.

Lay out 10 half-square triangle units, with the colors going the same direction – pink on the bottom, brown on the top. Sew together in a row and press.

Sew 2 strips to either side of the quilt, with the pink side sewn next to the center. Press.

Layout 12 of the half-square triangle blocks with the first 11 blocks the same as the sides, but the last block turned so the brown is on the bottom, pink on the top as shown in the quilt assembly diagram. Sew together in a row and press. Sew the strips to the top and bottom of the quilt, with the pink side sewn next to the center of the quilt, and press.

Finishing

Quilt as desired and bind.

ASSEMBLY DIAGRAM

GRANDMA'S TULIP GARDEN BAG

By Karlene Riggs

Finished Bag Size: 10 ½" x 10 ½" x 3 ½"

Fabric Requirements

- Scraps of browns, pinks and greens for the outside of the bag
- ½ yard brown fabric for the lining
- Scrap of batting about 10" x 11" for the bottom of the bag

Additional Supplies

- 2 – 8 ½" unfinished blocks from Grandma's Tulip Garden on page 60 or 2 blocks of your choice that are 8 ½" unfinished.
- ¾ yard fusible heavyweight interfacing, such as Pellon
- Handles such as Everything Mary, Braided Microfiber Handles
- 3 ¾" x 10 ¾" Template Plastic (for the bottom of the bag)

Cutting

- From the brown scraps, cut:
    - 4 – 6 ¾" squares. Cut each in half diagonally.
    - 3 – 5" squares
- From the pink scraps, cut:
    - 3 – 5" squares
- From the lining fabric cut:
    - 1 – 2" x 18" strip for the handle loops
    - 1 – 11 ¾" x 30 ½" rectangle
    - 1 – 4 ½" x 11 ½" rectangle for the outer base
    - 1 – 5" x 12" rectangle for the inner base
- From the interfacing, cut:
    - 1 – 11 ¾" x 30 ½" rectangle

Sewing

Bag Front and Back

Sew each of the 4 – 6 ¾" triangles to all sides of one 8 ½" unfinished block as shown. Press and trim block to 11 ¾". Repeat with the remaining block and triangles.

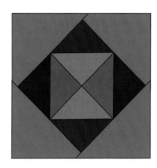

Bag Sides

Match 1 pink and 1 brown square with right sides together, draw a line down the center of the pink square diagonally. Sew ¼" on both sides of the drawn line.

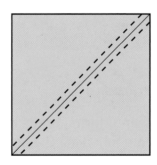

Cut apart on the drawn line. Press open and trim to 4 ¼" square. Repeat with all of the brown and pink 5" squares to make 6 blocks.

Referring to the diagram, sew together the half-square triangle blocks into 2 rows of 3 each. These units will measure 4 ¼" x 11 ¾".

Lay the bag out with 1 side panel, the front block, 1 side panel, and the back block. Sew together and press well. This should measure 11 ¾" x 30 ½".

Lining and Interfacing

Press the fusible interfacing to the back of the bag and the lining following the manufacturer's directions. Make sure the bag and the lining are the same size or you will have trouble sewing them together.

Note: I like to use the heavyweight interfacing on my bags because it makes the bag very stiff and it stands up on its own. But, if you choose not to use it, the bag will be easier to turn right side out during construction.

Fold the handle loop fabric in half lengthwise and press. Unfold, fold the sides to the pressed fold, fold in half again and press. The loop strips should measure ½" x 18".

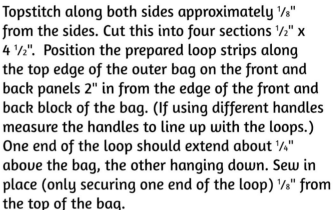

Topstitch along both sides approximately ⅛" from the sides. Cut this into four sections ½" x 4 ½". Position the prepared loop strips along the top edge of the outer bag on the front and back panels 2" in from the edge of the front and back block of the bag. (If using different handles measure the handles to line up with the loops.) One end of the loop should extend about ¼" above the bag, the other hanging down. Sew in place (only securing one end of the loop) ⅛" from the top of the bag.

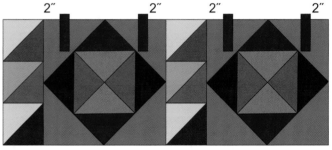

Fold the bag with right sides together and sew the side seam. Repeat this step for the lining.

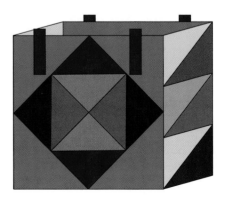

Press the seams open and turn the outer bag right sides out. Pull the lining down over the main section of the bag so they are right sides together with the side seams and upper raw edges aligned, pin in place, if this is not smooth and even adjust one of the side seams of the bag or lining now, then stitch around the top edge.

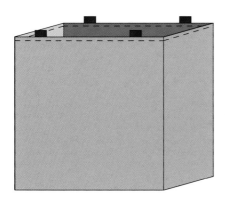

I like to open this up now and press it. It will give the top of your bag a more finished and nicer look. Now fold the lining down inside the bag, press well and topstitch along the top of the bag about ¼" from the edge. Pin the lining and outer bag together around the base and stitch a scant ¼" from the bottom raw edge with matching thread to secure the layers together. Clip along the bottom edge between each panel along the center stitching line, within the ¼" seam allowance.

Turn the bag wrong sides out, pin the 4 ½" x 11 ½" outer base to the bag right sides together. Match the corners of the base with the bottom of the outer bag so the clipped areas open up at the corners then stitch the base in place. (This is the hardest part, and there are no bag police checking your work, just do the best you can, and it will look great.)

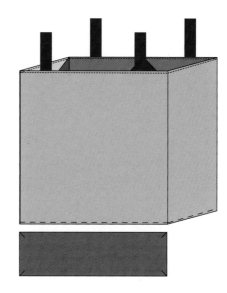

Wrap the template plastic with the batting, hand stitch the batting in place around the plastic so it won't bunch up. With the bag still wrong sides out and the bag upside down, lay the plastic on the bottom of the bag. Trim the plastic if you need to so it fits inside the seam allowance on the bottom of the bag. Using the 5" x 12" inner base, press in ¼" all the around the edges. Lay this piece of fabric onto the base of the bag, enclosing the plastic and batting and hand stitch all around. Turn the bag right sides out and this piece you just hand stitched will be on the inside, bottom of the bag.

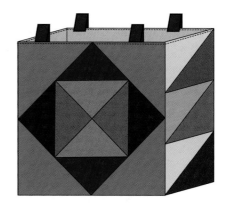

Thread the handle loops through the handles. Trim the loops if they are too long. Tuck under the end about ¼" and top stitch in place on the top, inside of the bag, going right over the topstitching on the top of the bag (my loops were about ½" long from the top of the bag to the fold). Repeat for all four handles to finish.

SPRING BASKETS

By Amy Smart

Finished Quilt Size: 41" x 54"
Finished Block Size: 6 ½" x 9"

"I love to watch the mountains out my front window as they change with the seasons. The snow starting to melt and the colors changing to green is such a hopeful sign that winter is done and warm temperatures are on their way!"

- AMY SMART

Fabric Requirements

- 13 fat quarters of assorted pastel colors for the basket blocks. You may also use 7 – $\frac{1}{3}$ yard pieces or assorted scraps
- $\frac{1}{4}$ yard pink print for the inner border
- $\frac{2}{3}$ yard yellow print for the outer border
- 2 $\frac{3}{4}$ yards for the backing
- $\frac{1}{2}$ yard for the binding
- 47" x 60" piece of batting

Additional Supplies
- Freezer paper

Cutting

- From the 13 fat quarters, cut 25 – 10" x 12" squares, one for each basket. You can get 2 – 10" x 12" blocks from a fat quarter or 4 from $\frac{1}{3}$ yard of fabric.

- From the pink inner border fabric, cut 5 – 1 $\frac{1}{4}$" strips x the width of the fabric.

- From yellow outer border fabric, cut 5 – 4" strips x the width of the fabric.

- From binding fabric, cut 5 – 2 $\frac{1}{2}$" strips x the width of the fabric.

Blocks

The templates are found on pages 93-94.

Trace the basket pattern 6 times onto the dull side of the freezer paper. Be sure to label each piece as they are labeled on the pattern. Press the traced pattern on top of a stack of 4 or 5 fabric blocks. You will need 25 total. Rotary cut through the marked lines of the pattern, using a quilting ruler to keep your lines straight. Leave an extra ½" of fabric around the block pieces to have extra fabric when squaring up the blocks.

Sewing

Shuffle the fabrics by moving basket pieces (bottom plus handle pieces) replacing original basket pieces inside contrasting background fabrics. Contrasting fabric will make the baskets show up nicely in each block.

To begin reassembling the baskets, start with Section A and sew the pieces together in numerical order as shown in the diagrams. The pieces will not match up perfectly and there will be some pieces longer or shorter than the new piece they are being sewn to. This is normal and edges will be squared-off eventually. Repeat the process assembling Section B pieces.

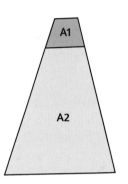

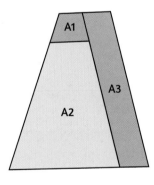

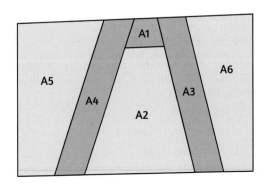

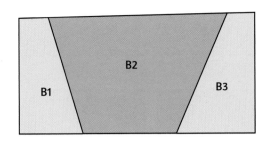

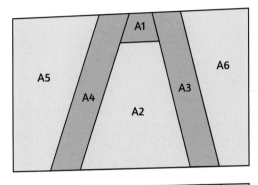

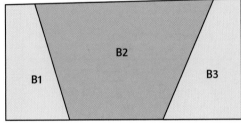

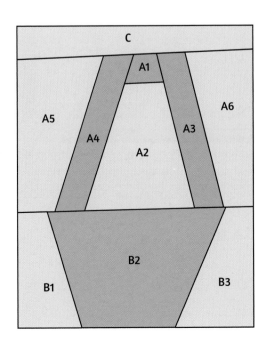

Next, square off edges of top and bottoms of Sections A and B. These baskets are supposed to be imperfect and a little bit off-kilter. Don't stress about squaring things up perfectly at this point. You just need straight edges to sew the three sections together.

Sew Section A to Section B. Be sure to center the basket handles above the base. Add Section C to the top. After the entire block is sewn together, square up the block to 7" x 9 ½." Repeat to make 25 blocks.

Top Assembly

Referring to the assembly diagram on page 74, lay out the quilt in 5 rows of 5 blocks each. Assemble the blocks in order by rows and then assemble the 5 rows together.

Borders

Measure the quilt top center from top to bottom. Sew the inner border strips together and trim to that length. Sew to each side and press. Measure across the top again from side to side and sew the remaining strips that length. Sew one to the top and one to the bottom. Press.

Measure the quilt top center from side to side. Sew the outer border strips together and trim to that length. Sew to each side and press. Measure across the top again from side to side and sew the remaining strips that length. Sew one to the top and one to the bottom. Press.

Finishing

Quilt as desired and bind.

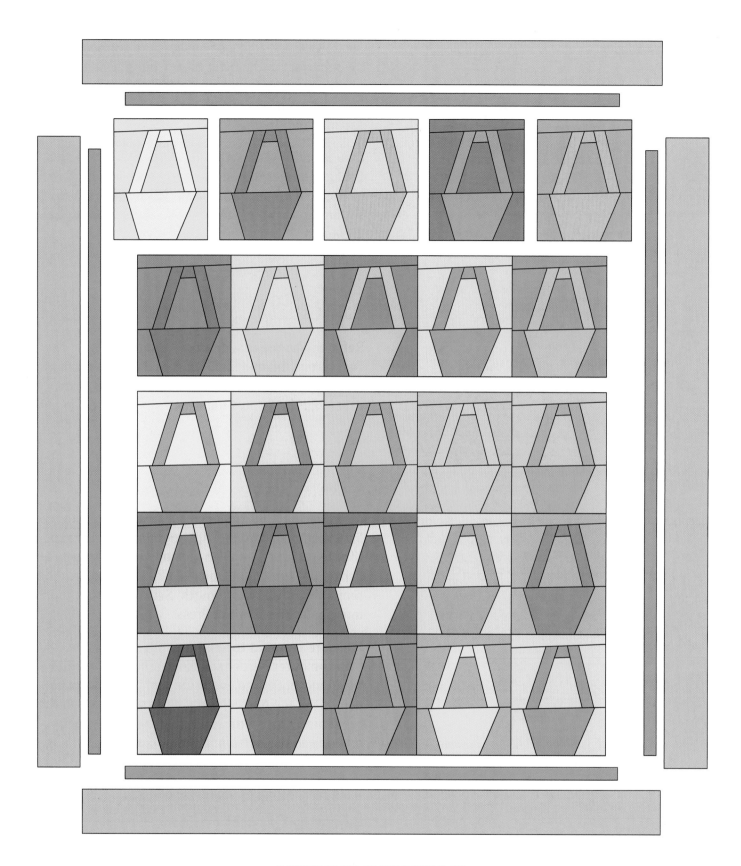

ASSEMBLY DIAGRAM

MINI CHICK PILLOWS
By Margie Ullery

Pillow Size: 6"

"I grew up in central California where you had to drive for hours to get to the mountains. Now I live with the mountains in my backyard, and I love it! When spring comes to our mountains you can see and feel them wake up. What a great place to live."

— MARCIE ULLERY

Fabric Requirements

- Scrap of white fabric for background
- Assorted scraps for chick appliqué
- Scrap of print fabric for pillow backing

Additional Supplies
- 1 yard medium rickrack per pillow
- 2 – ⅛" buttons for the chick eyes per pillow
- Fusible web
- Pillow stuffing

Cutting

- From the background fabric, cut 1 – 6 ½" square.

- From the pillow backing fabric, cut 1 – 6 ½" square.

- From the rickrack, cut 4 – 7 ½" strips.

Sewing

The templates are found on page 88.

Using the template, trace each chick section onto the fusible web. Roughly cut out each section and iron it onto the back of your chick scraps following the manufacturer's instructions. Cut out each piece on the line. Place all the parts of the chick centered on the right side of the 6 ½" background fabric as shown. Press. Blanket stitch or zigzag around the appliqué pieces. Sew on the two buttons for the little chick's eyes.

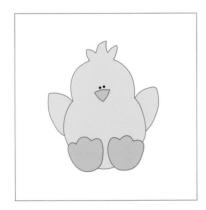

Center one 7 ½" rickrack strip along the edge of the right side of the background square as shown. Stitch down the center of the rickrack. Before you come to the end of the strip, insert the second strip along the next edge as shown and continue stitching. Continue in this manner sewing the rickrack around all sides of the background square.

Place the square with the 6 ½" pillow backing fabric with right sides together. Starting at the side of one edge as shown, sew along the seam line that is there from sewing the rick rack on. Don't worry about what the seam allowance is. Leave an opening to turn the pillow right side out.

Trim the excess rickrack from the corners of the square, and clip the corners for easier turning. Turn the pillow right side out.

Finishing

Stuff the pillow and slip stitch the opening shut.

Stepping Into Spring

Note: Reverse the pattern if using fusible web.

Attach on dotted line

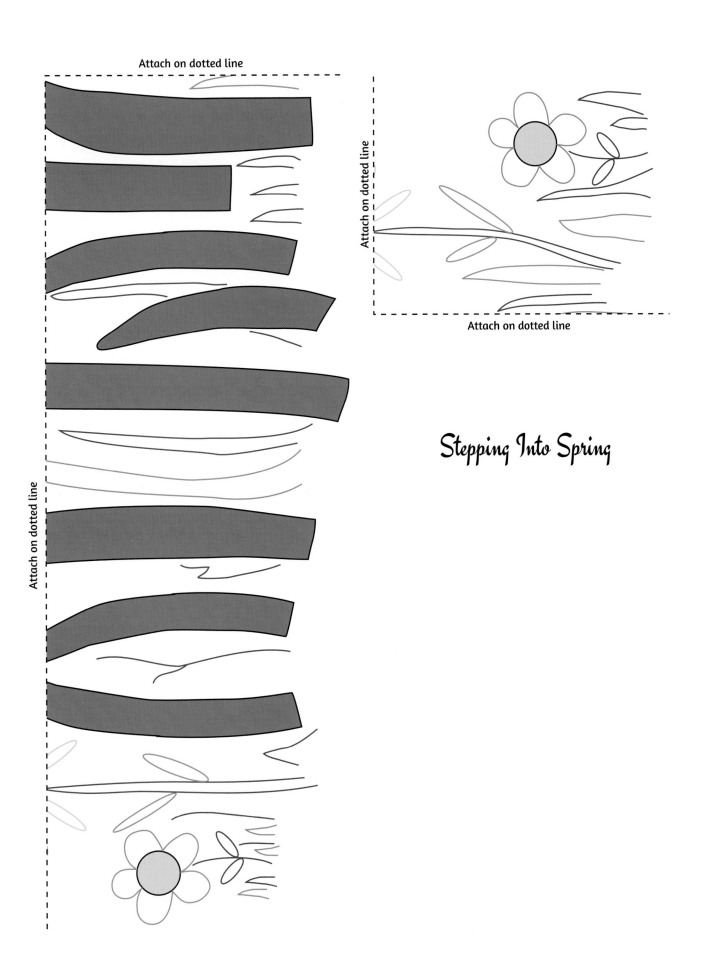

Attach on dotted line

Attach on dotted line

Attach on dotted line

Stepping Into Spring

Scrambled Eggs

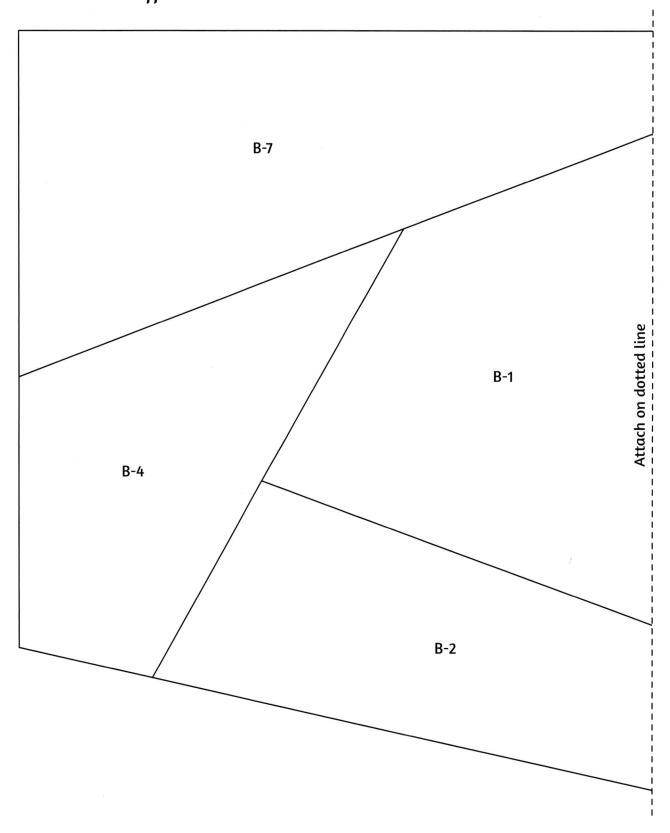

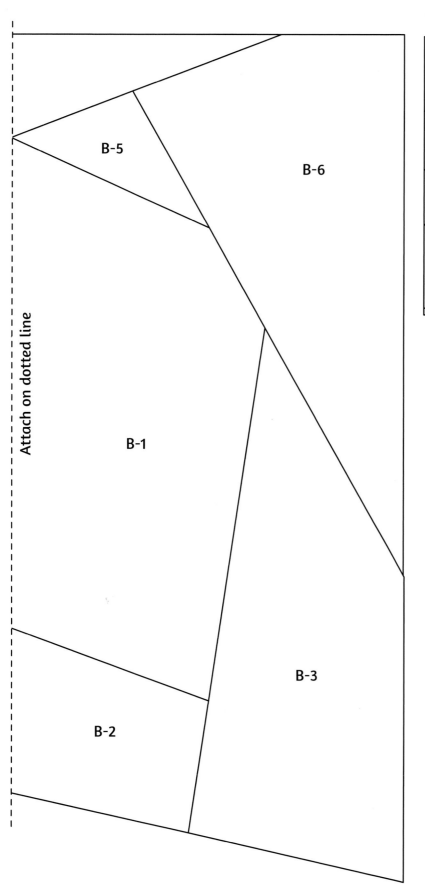

Attach on dotted line

B-5

B-6

B-1

B-3

B-2

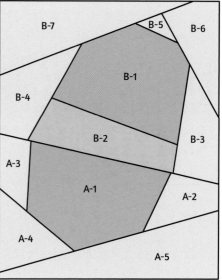

B-7   B-5   B-6
B-1
B-4
B-2   B-3
A-3
A-1   A-2
A-4
A-5

Scrambled Eggs

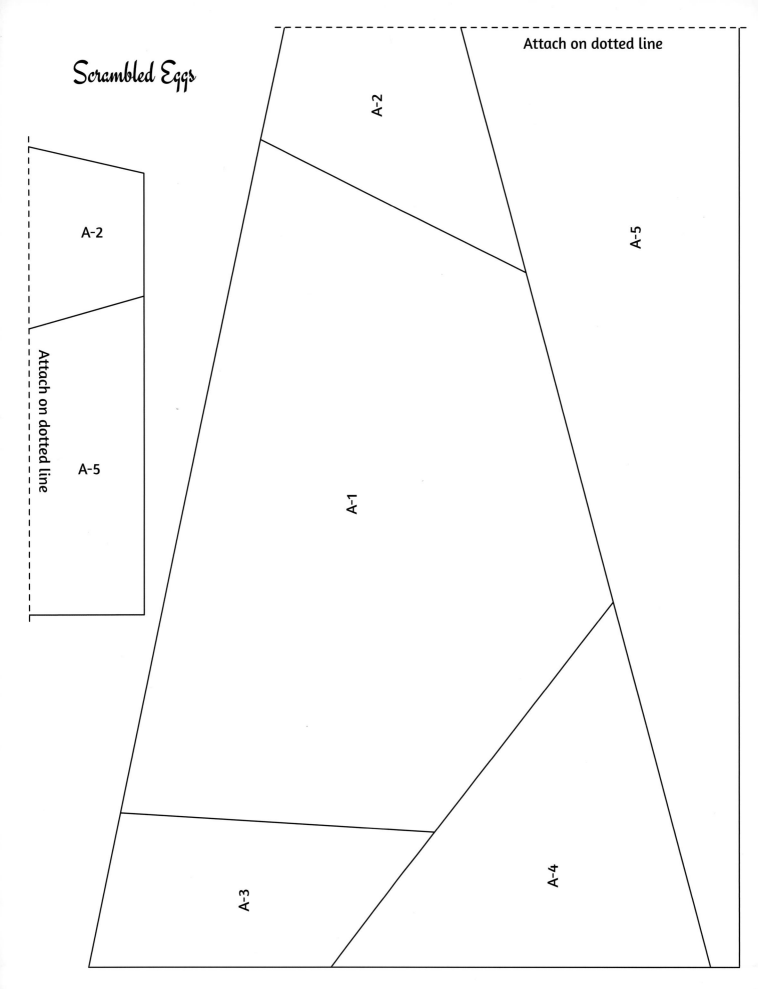

Scrambled Eggs

Attach on dotted line

A-2

A-2

A-5

Attach on dotted line

A-5

A-1

A-5

A-3

A-4

Attach on dotted line

True North

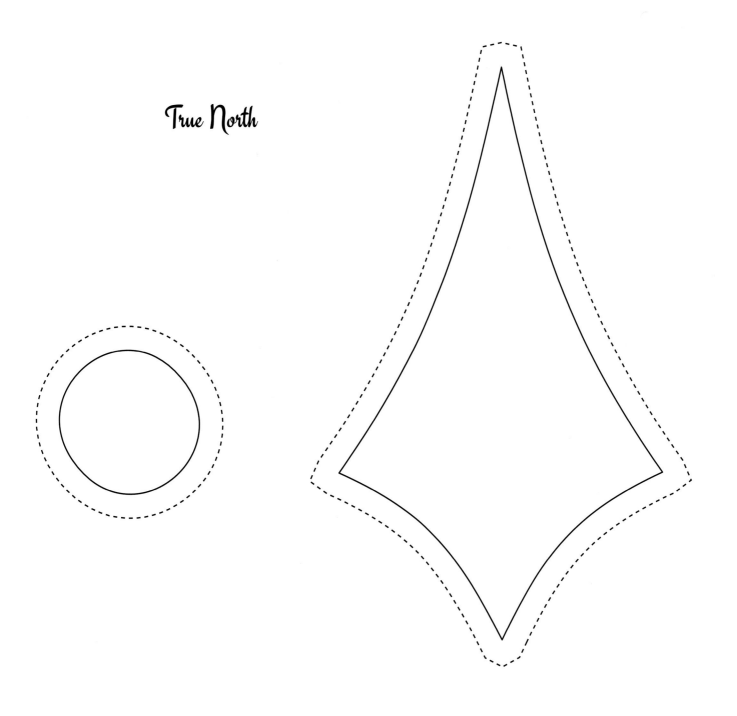

Spring Bouquet

First

Attach on dotted line

Attach on dotted line

Last

Attach on dotted line

Josefina

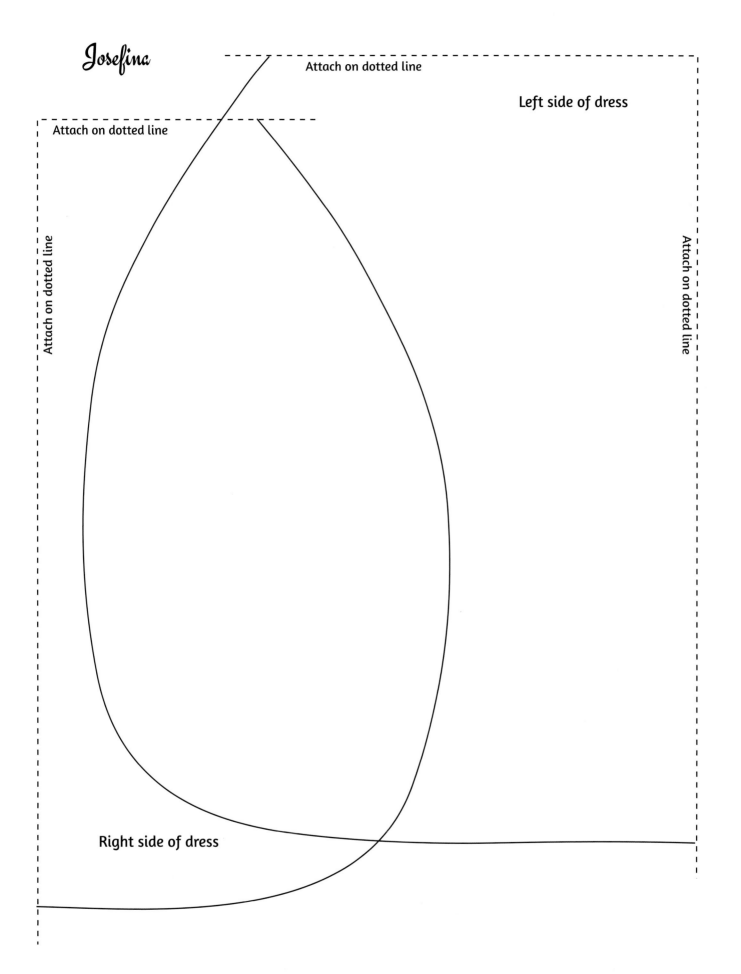

Attach on dotted line

Left side of dress

Attach on dotted line

Attach on dotted line

Attach on dotted line

Right side of dress

The Hills are Alive

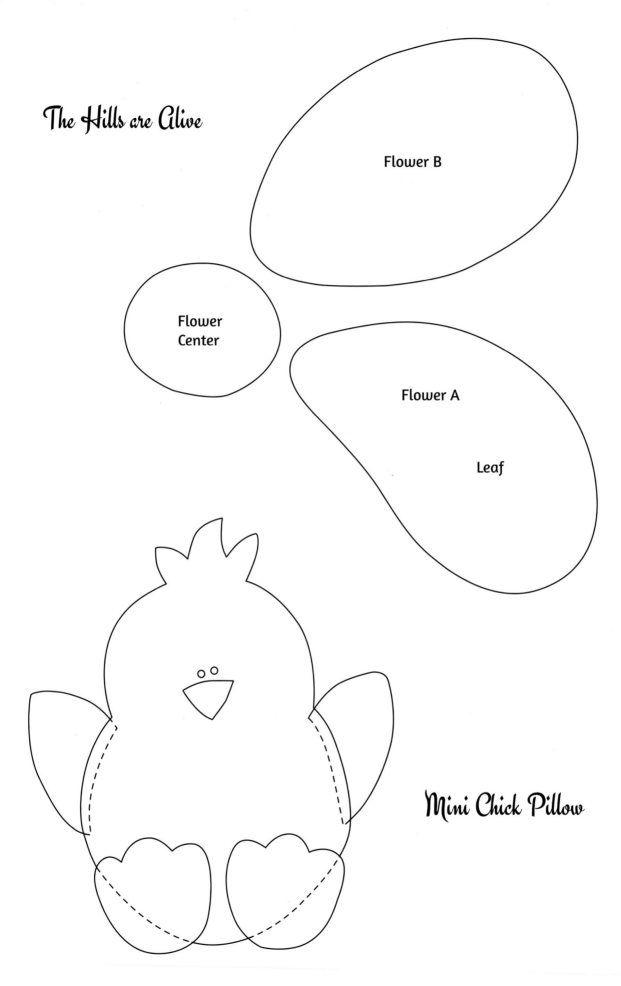

Flower B

Flower
Center

Flower A

Leaf

Mini Chick Pillow

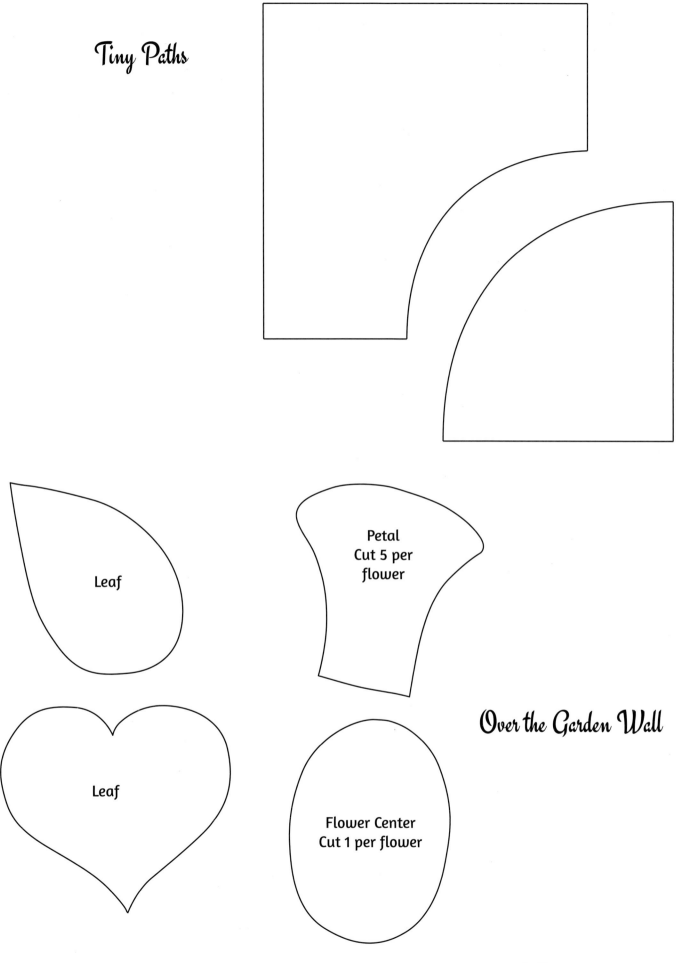

Tiny Paths

Leaf

Leaf

Petal
Cut 5 per
flower

Over the Garden Wall

Flower Center
Cut 1 per flower

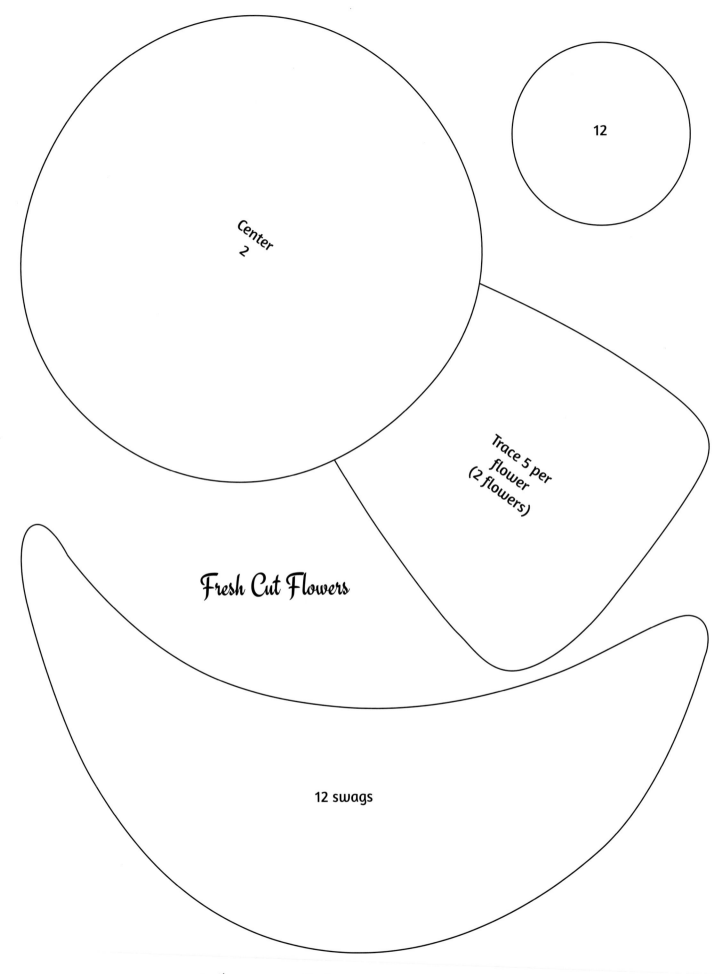

Center
2

12

Trace 5 per
flower
(2 flowers)

Fresh Cut Flowers

12 swags

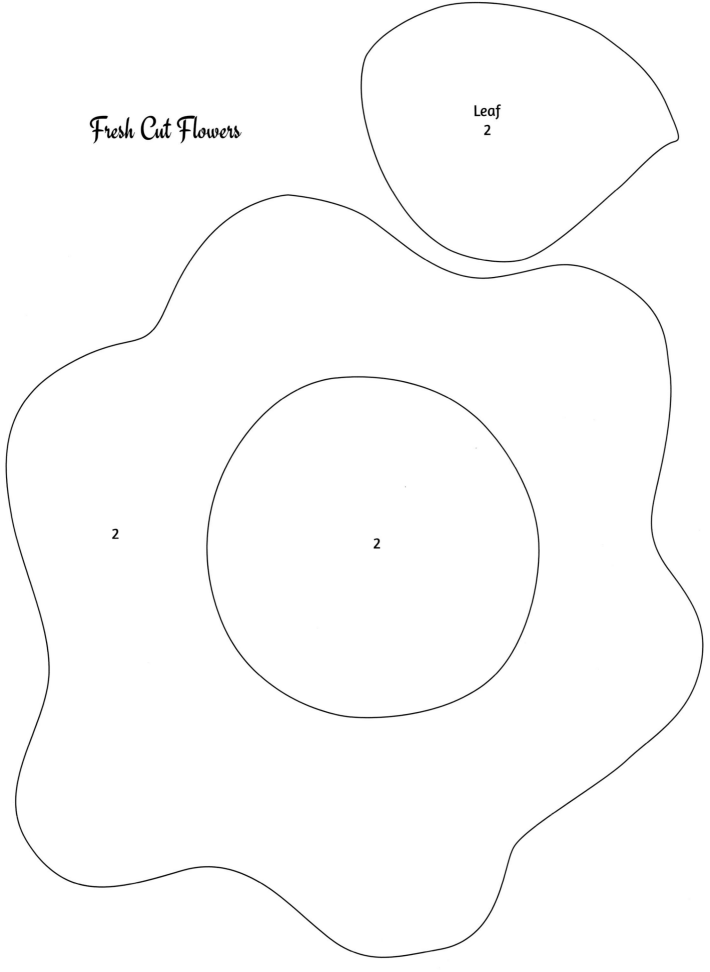

Fresh Cut Flowers

Leaf
2

2

2

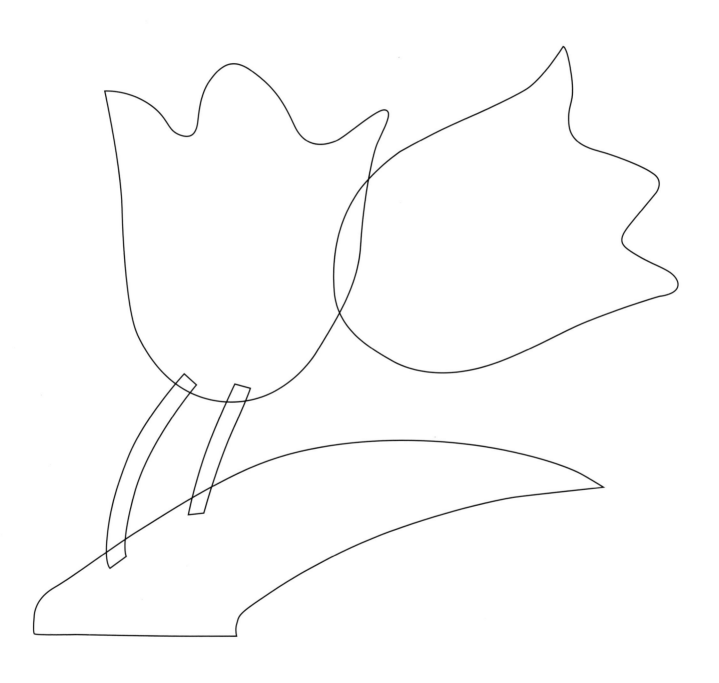

Spring Baskets

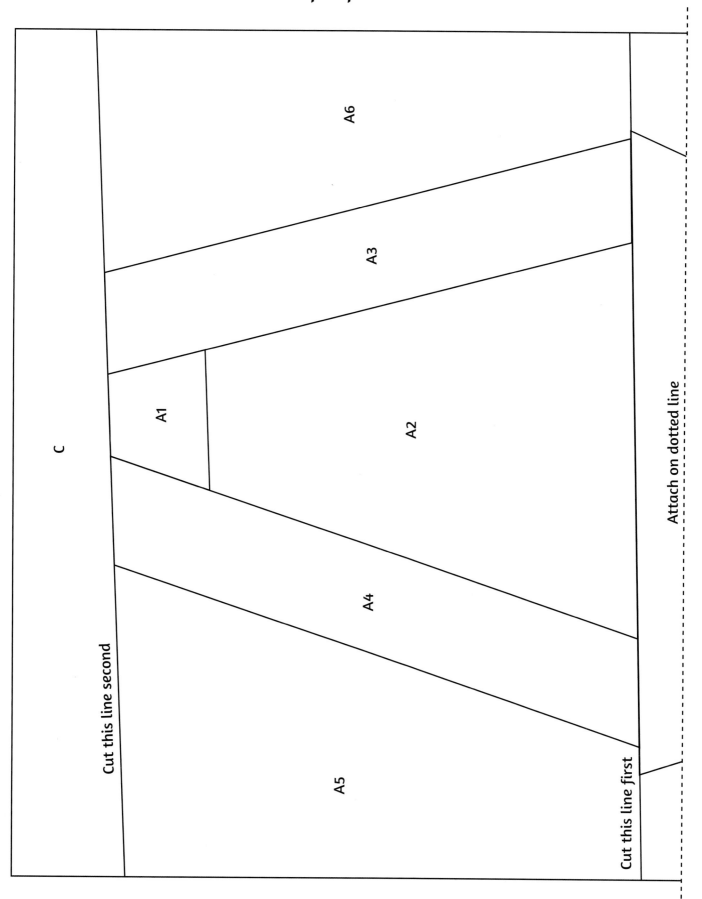

C

A6

A3

A1

A2

A4

A5

Cut this line second

Cut this line first

Attach on dotted line

Spring Baskets

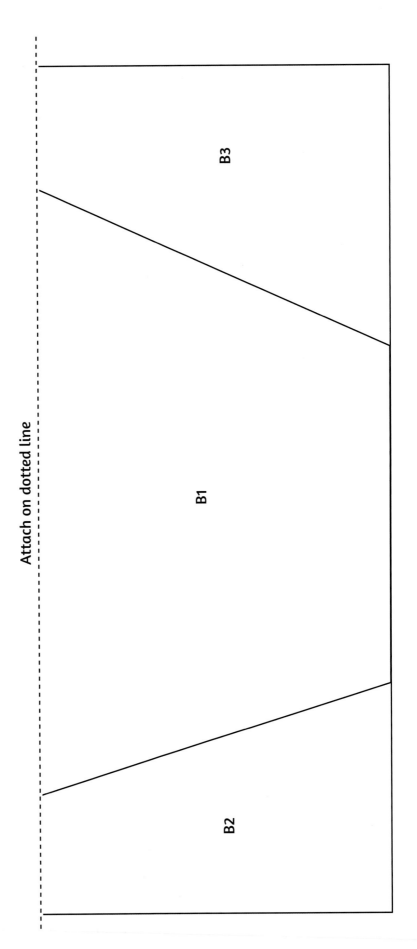

Attach on dotted line

B3

B1

B2

Other Kansas City Star Quilts Books

One Piece at a Time by Kansas City Star Books – 1999

More Kansas City Star Quilts by Kansas City Star Books – 2000

Outside the Box: Hexagon Patterns from The Kansas City Star by Edie McGinnis – 2001

Prairie Flower: A Year on the Plains by Barbara Brackman – 2001

The Sister Blocks by Edie McGinnis – 2001

Kansas City Quiltmakers by Doug Worgul – 2001

O'Glory: Americana Quilt Blocks from The Kansas City Star by Edie McGinnis – 2001

Hearts and Flowers: Hand Appliqué from Start to Finish by Kathy Delaney – 2002

Roads and Curves Ahead: A Trip Through Time with Classic Kansas City Star *Quilt Blocks* by Edie McGinnis – 2002

Celebration of American Life: Appliqué Patterns Honoring a Nation and Its People by Barb Adams and Alma Allen – 2002

Women of Grace & Charm: A Quilting Tribute to the Women Who Served in World War II by Barb Adams and Alma Allen – 2003

A Heartland Album: More Techniques in Hand Appliqué by Kathy Delaney – 2003

Quilting a Poem: Designs Inspired by America's Poets by Frances Kite and Deb Rowden – 2003

Carolyn's Paper Pieced Garden: Patterns for Miniature and Full-Sized Quilts by Carolyn Cullinan McCormick – 2003

Friendships in Bloom: Round Robin Quilts by Marjorie Nelson and Rebecca Nelson-Zerfas – 2003

Baskets of Treasures: Designs Inspired by Life Along the River by Edie McGinnis – 2003

Heart & Home: Unique American Women and the Houses that Inspire by Kathy Schmitz – 2003

Women of Design: Quilts in the Newspaper by Barbara Brackman – 2004

The Basics: An Easy Guide to Beginning Quiltmaking by Kathy Delaney – 2004

Four Block Quilts: Echoes of History, Pieced Boldly & Appliquéd Freely by Terry Clothier Thompson – 2004

No Boundaries: Bringing Your Fabric Over the Edge by Edie McGinnis – 2004

Horn of Plenty for a New Century by Kathy Delaney – 2004

Quilting the Garden by Barb Adams and Alma Allen – 2004

Stars All Around Us: Quilts and Projects Inspired by a Beloved Symbol by Cherie Ralston – 2005

Quilters' Stories: Collecting History in the Heart of America by Deb Rowden – 2005

Libertyville: Where Liberty Dwells, There is My Country by Terry Clothier Thompson – 2005

Sparkling Jewels, Pearls of Wisdom by Edie McGinnis – 2005

Grapefruit Juice and Sugar: Bold Quilts Inspired by Grandmother's Legacy by Jenifer Dick – 2005

Home Sweet Home by Barb Adams and Alma Allen – 2005

Patterns of History: The Challenge Winners by Kathy Delaney – 2005

My Quilt Stories by Debra Rowden – 2005

Quilts in Red and Green and the Women Who Made Them by Nancy Hornback and Terry Clothier Thompson – 2006

Hard Times, Splendid Quilts: A 1930s Celebration, Paper Piecing from The Kansas City Star by Carolyn Cullinan McCormick – 2006

Art Nouveau Quilts for the 21st Century by Bea Oglesby – 2006

Designer Quilts: Great Projects from Moda's Best Fabric Artists – 2006

Birds of a Feather by Barb Adams and Alma Allen – 2006

Feedsacks! Beautiful Quilts from Humble Beginnings by Edie McGinnis – 2006

Kansas Spirit: Historical Quilt Blocks and the Saga of the Sunflower State by Jeanne Poore – 2006

Bold Improvisation: Searching for African-American Quilts – The Heffley Collection by Scott Heffley – 2007

The Soulful Art of African-American Quilts: Nineteen Bold, Improvisational Projects by Sonie Ruffin – 2007

Alphabet Quilts: Letters for All Ages by Bea Oglesby – 2007

Beyond the Basics: A Potpourri of Quiltmaking Techniques by Kathy Delaney – 2007

Golden's Journal: 20 Sampler Blocks Honoring Prairie Farm Life by Christina DeArmond, Eula Lang and Kaye Spitzli – 2007

Borderland in Butternut and Blue: A Sampler Quilt to Recall the Civil War Along the Kansas/Missouri Border by Barbara Brackman – 2007

Come to the Fair: Quilts that Celebrate State Fair Traditions by Edie McGinnis – 2007

Cotton and Wool: Miss Jump's Farewell by Linda Brannock – 2007

You're Invited! Quilts and Homes to Inspire by Barb Adams and Alma Allen of Blackbird Designs – 2007

Portable Patchwork: Who Says You Can't Take it With You? by Donna Thomas – 2008

Quilts for Rosie: Paper Piecing Patterns from the '40s by Carolyn Cullinan McCormick – 2008

Fruit Salad: Appliqué Designs for Delicious Quilts by Bea Oglesby – 2008

Red, Green and Beyond by Nancy Hornback and Terry Clothier Thompson – 2008

A Dusty Garden Grows by Terry Clothier Thompson – 2008

We Gather Together: A Harvest of Quilts by Jan Patek – 2008

With These Hands: 19th Century-Inspired Primitive Projects for Your Home by Maggie Bonanomi – 2008

As the Cold Wind Blows by Barb Adams and Alma Allen of Blackbird Designs – 2008

Caring for Your Quilts: Textile Conservation, Repair and Storage by Hallye Bone – 2008

The Circuit Rider's Quilt: An Album Quilt Honoring a Beloved Minister by Jenifer Dick – 2008

Embroidered Quilts: From Hands and Hearts by Christina DeArmond, Eula Lang and Kaye Spitzli – 2008

Reminiscing: A Whimsicals Collection by Terri Degenkolb – 2008

Scraps and Shirttails: Reuse, Re-purpose and Recycle! The Art of Green Quilting by Bonnie Hunter – 2008

Flora Botanica: Quilts from the Spencer Museum of Art by Barbara Brackman – 2009

Making Memories: Simple Quilts from Cherished Clothing by Deb Rowden – 2009

Pots de Fleurs: A Garden of Applique Techniques by Kathy Delaney – 2009

Wedding Ring, Pickle Dish and More: Paper Piecing Curves by Carolyn McCormick – 2009

The Graceful Garden: A Jacobean Fantasy Quilt by Denise Sheehan – 2009

My Stars: Patterns from The Kansas City Star, Volume I – 2009

Opening Day: 14 Quilts Celebrating the Life and Times of Negro Leagues Baseball by Sonie Ruffin – 2009

St. Louis Stars: Nine Unique Quilts that Spark by Toby Lischko – 2009

Whimsyland: Be Cre8ive with Lizzie B by Liz & Beth Hawkins – 2009

Cradle to Cradle by Barbara Jones of Quilt Soup – 2009

Pick of the Seasons: Quilts to Inspire You Through the Year by Tammy Johnson and Avis Shirer of Joined at the Hip – 2009

Across the Pond: Projects Inspired by Quilts of the British Isles by Bettina Havig – 2009

Artful Bras: Hooters, Melons and Boobs, Oh My! A Quilt Guild's Fight Against Breast Cancer by the Quilters of South Carolina - 2009

Flags of the American Revolution by Jan Patek – 2009

Get Your Stitch on Route 66: Quilts from the Mother Road by Christina DeArmond, Eula Lang and Kaye Spitzli from Of One Mind – 2009

Gone to Texas: Quilts from a Pioneer Woman's Journals by Betsy Chutchian – 2009

Juniper and Mistletoe: A Forest of Applique by Karla Menaugh and Barbara Brackman - 2009

My Stars II: Patterns from The Kansas City Star, Volume II – 2009

Nature's Offerings: Primitive Projects Inspired by the Four Seasons by Maggie Bonanomi – 2009

Quilts of the Golden West: Mining the History of the Gold and Silver Rush by Cindy Brick – 2009

Women of Influence: 12 Leaders of the Suffrage Movement by Sarah Maxwell and Dolores Smith of Homestead Hearth – 2009

Adventures with Leaders and Enders: Make More Quilts in Less Time! by Bonnie Hunter – 2010

A Bird in Hand: Folk Art Projects Inspired by Our Feathered Friends by Renee Plains – 2010

Feedsack Secrets: Fashion from Hard Times by Gloria Nixon – 2010

Greetings from Tucsadelphia: Travel-Inspired Projects from Lizzie B Cre8ive by Liz & Beth Hawkins – 2010

The Big Book of Bobbins: Fun, Quilty Cartoons by Julia Icenogle – 2010

Country Inn by Barb Adams and Alma Allen of Blackbird Designs – 2010

My Stars III: Patterns from The Kansas City Star, Volume III – 2010

Piecing the Past: Vintage Quilts Recreated by Kansas Troubles by Lynne Hagmeier – 2010

Stitched Together: Fresh Projects and Ideas for Group Quilting by Jill Finley – 2010

A Case for Adventures by Katie Kerr – 2010

A Little Porch Time: Quilts with a Touch of Southern Hospitality by Lynda Hall – 2010

Circles: Floral Applique in the Round by Bea Oglesby – 2010

Comfort Zone: More Primitive Projects for You and Your Home by Maggie Bonanomi – 2010

Leaving Baltimore: A Prairie Album Quilt by Christina DeArmond, Eula Lang and Kaye Spitzli from Of One Mind – 2010

Like Mother, Like Daughter: Two Generations of Quilts by Karen Witt and Erin Witt – 2010

Sew Into Sports: Quilts for the Fans in Your Life by Barbara Brackman – 2010

Under the Stars by Cherie Ralston – 2010

A Path to the Civil War: Aurelia's Journey Quilt by Sarah Maxwell and Dolores Smith of Homestead Hearth – 2010

Across the Wide Missouri: A Quilt Reflecting Life on the Frontier by Edie McGinnis and Jan Patek – 2010

Cottage Charm: Cozy Quilts and Cross Stitch Projects by Dawn Heese – 2010

My Stars IV: Patterns from The Kansas City Star, Volume IV – 2010

Roaring Through the 20s: Paper Pieced Quilts from the Flapper Era by Carolyn Cullinan McCormick – 2010

Happy Birthday Kansas by Barbara Jones – 2011

Simply Charming: Small Scrap Quilts of Yesteryear – 2011

Flower Dance: Beautiful Applique Using No-Fail Techniques by Hallye Bone – 2011

Scraps and Shirttails II: Continuing the Art of Quilting Green by Bonnie Hunter – 2011

Stars: A Study of 19th Century Star Quilts by American Quilt Study Group – 2011

My Stars V: Patterns from the Kansas City Star, Volume V – 2011

Home on the Plains: Quilts and the Sod House Experience by Kathleen Moore and Stephanie Whitson – 2011

Table Talk: Runners, Toppers and Family Treats by Gudrun Erla – 2011

Four Seasons at Minglewood by Debbie Roberts – 2011

Confederates in the Cornfield: Civil War Quilts from Davis County, Iowa by Edie McGinnis – 2011

Santaland: A Bright Collection of Holiday Quilts and Crafts by Brian Grubb with Of One Mind – 2011

Some Kind of Wonderful by Anni Downs – 2011

Fruitful Hands by Jacquelynne Steves – 2011

Be Merry: Quilt Projects for Your Holiday Home by Martha Walker – 2011

A Baker's Dozen: 13 Kitchen Quilts from American Jane – 2011

Graceful Rhapsody: A Quilted Paisley Block-of-the-Month by Denise Sheehan – 2011

History Repeated: Block Exchange Quilts by the 19th Century Patchwork Divas by Betsy Chutchian and Carol Staehle – 2011

A Schoolgirl's Work: Samplers from the Spencer Museum of Art by Barb Adams and Alma Allen – 2011

Stitches from the Schoolhouse: Projects Inspired by Classrooms of the Past by Renee Plains – 2011

Quilt Retro: 11 Designs to Make Your Own by Jenifer Dick – 2011

Faithful and Devoted: To My Adelaide – A Quilted Love Story by Sarah Maxwell and Delores Smith – 2011

Buttonwood Farm: 19 New Primitive Projects by Maggie Bonanomi – 2011

Taupe Inspirations: Modern Quilts Inspired by Japanese Taupes by Kylie Irvine – 2011

Victory Girls: Patriotic Quilts and Rugs of WWII by Polly Minick and Laurie Simpson – 2011

My Stars VI: Patterns from The Kanas City Star, Volume VI – 2011

A Year of Cozy Comforts: Quilts and Projects for Every Season by Dawn Heese – 2012

Story Time: Picture Quilts to Stir a Child's Imagination by Kim Gaddy – 2012

A Bountiful Life: An Adaptation of the Bird of Paradise Quilt Top in the American Folk Art Museum by Karen Mowery – 2012

American Summer: Seaside-Inspired Rugs & Quilts by Polly Minick – 2012

Project Books

Fan Quilt Memories by Jeanne Poore – 2000

Santa's Parade of Nursery Rhymes by Jeanne Poore – 2001

As the Crow Flies by Edie McGinnis – 2007

Sweet Inspirations by Pam Manning – 2007

Quilts Through the Camera's Eye by Terry Clothier Thompson – 2007

Louisa May Alcott: Quilts of Her Life, Her Work, Her Heart by Terry Clothier Thompson – 2008

The Lincoln Museum Quilt: A Reproduction for Abe's Frontier Cabin by Barbara Brackman and Deb Rowden – 2008

Dinosaurs - Stomp, Chomp and Roar by Pam Manning – 2008

Carrie Hall's Sampler: Favorite Blocks from a Classic Pattern Collection by Barbara Brackman – 2008

Just Desserts: Quick Quilts Using Pre-cut Fabrics by Edie McGinnis – 2009

Christmas at Home: Quilts for Your Holiday Traditions by Christina DeArmond, Eula Lang and Kaye Spitzli from Of One Mind - 2009

Geese in the Rose Garden by Dawn Heese – 2009

Winter Trees by Jane Kennedy – 2009

Ruby Red Dots: Fanciful Circle-Inspired Designs by Sheri M. Howard – 2009

Backyard Blooms: A Month by Month Garden Sampler by Barbara Jones of QuiltSoup – 2010

Not Your Grandmother's Quilt: An Applique Twist on Traditional Pieced Blocks by Sheri M. Howard – 2010

A Second Helping of Desserts: More Sweet Quilts Using Pre-cut Fabric by Edie McGinnis – 2010

Café au Lait: Paper Piece a Rocky Road to Kansas by Edie McGinnis – 2010

Border Garden by Lynne Hagmeier – 2010

From the Bedroom to the Barnyard: A 9-Block Sampler Honoring Barn Quilts – 2010

Picnic Park by Barbara Jones of QuiltSoup – 2010

Book of Days by Maggie Bonanomi – 2011

Hot Off the Press Patterns

Cabin in the Stars by Jan Patek – 2009

Arts & Crafts Sunflower by Barbara Brackman – 2009

Birthday Cake by Barbara Brackman – 2009

Strawberry Thief by Barbara Brackman – 2009

French Wrens by Dawn Heese - 2010

Queen Bees Mysteries

Murders on Elderberry Road by Sally Goldenbaum – 2003

A Murder of Taste by Sally Goldenbaum – 2004

Murder on a Starry Night by Sally Goldenbaum – 2005

Dog-Gone Murder by Marnette Falley – 2008

DVD Projects

The Kansas City Stars: A Quilting Legacy – 2008